Rising Above

ENRON

AN INSIDER VIEW OF THE COLLAPSE,
AND HOW TWELVE PEOPLE USED IT
TO TRANSFORM THEIR LIVES.

CAREY FALTER

PRINTED IN THE UNITED STATES OF AMERICA

Visit the website: http://www.raenron.com for up to date contact information.

First edition published 2011.

Book interior and cover design by Tamian Wood, Beyond Design www.tamianwood.com

ISBN-10: 0984883444
ISBN-13: 978-0-9848834-4-8

CONTENTS

ACKNOWLEDGEMENTS

Rising Above Enron was a project that was challenging both professionally and personally. It is an accomplishment of a dream for me to write a book which highlights what makes the human spirit truly unique–overcoming adversity.

Everyone faces setbacks in life; what separates us is our attitude. While researching this book, I had the opportunity to speak to many people who worked for Enron. It was surprising to find that they all shared the same sentiment: that Enron was special and because of working there they will never be the same.

I would like to thank everyone who answered my calls and shared with me their Enron story. I have never spoken with so many amazing people that happened to work at the same company during the same period. You all are what made Enron great. Special thanks to the twelve who agreed to publicly share their story.

This book could not be possible without the love and support of many people. First and foremost I thank my husband Jason, thank you for believing in me and this project.

To my friend Brad, thank you for your honest and encouraging words. To my parents who always accepted those last minute requests to watch their grandson. To all my other friends and family members who offered their comforting words throughout the past year.

To Tamian Wood, thank you for listening to my requests and delivering far and above my expectations.

Thank you for God for giving me the idea, talents, and contacts that brought this book to life.

AUTHOR'S NOTE

This book is the product of countless hours of research on Enron and interviews with former employees. I consulted court documents, the Report of Investigation by the Special Investigations Committee of the Board of Enron, the Report of Investigation of Enron Corporation and Related Entities Regarding Federal Tax and Compensation Issues by the U.S. Congress Joint Committee on Taxation, and many other articles and books about Enron. This book briefly explains how Enron went bankrupt and primarily focuses on the personal experiences of twelve former employees.

Comments and stories are encouraged. Please visit the website www.raenron.com for submission instructions.

RISING ABOVE ENRON

INTRODUCTION

December 3, 2011 marked the ten-year anniversary of what was once the largest layoff in United States history. Never before had such a large corporation disintegrated in such a short period of time. With shock and fascination, America watched as 4,000 employees left the Enron building in downtown Houston with boxes of their belongings, facing an uncertain future.

What was so fascinating about Enron? Why study it today? The decisions that brought Enron down were based on greed and self-gratification. A disease that feeds on the idea that success is born overnight and the days of working hard are over. Money is not what defines a business or what measures its value; money is fleeting.

Enron was a morphed image of its original self; manipulated and transformed into a money making machine. Those who made up its true value, its employees, watched with excitement as the company steadily increased in value, quarter after quarter. Many were sold on the propaganda that everything Enron touched turned to gold. Why would they invest their money anywhere else when Enron was such a sure thing?

As the media cameras rolled, America watched as employees left the only job they ever loved. As the trial unfolded and the true scandals were revealed, interest quickly shifted to the sexier side of the story. More attention was paid to the private lives of its executives than to the personal struggles of its former employees.

As time moved on and bigger layoffs captured our attention, those former employees picked up and moved on. For them, there was little time to be spent worrying about how Enron collapsed; they were more focused on paying the mortgage and planning a new retirement.

In an effort to catch you, the reader, up on why this story is significant, I invite you to read a concise version of what essentially brought Enron down. This brief history will help frame some of the specific references made by those who shared their Enron experiences. If you desire to learn more about Enron and its sordid past, I invite you to check out many of the books which focus solely on that very topic.

THE BEGINNING OF ENRON

Enron came to be because InterNorth, a major natural gas company out of Omaha, Nebraska, merged with Houston Natural Gas (HNG). Shortly after the merger, Kenneth Lay became the CEO and Chairman of InterNorth/HNG and moved the headquarters to Houston.

One of the key players in Enron's demise is Jeffrey Skilling. He came on board on August 1, 1990 after working for many years as a business consultant to Enron. He petitioned the U.S. Securities and Exchange Commission and won approval to begin using Mark-to-Market accounting.

Mark-to-Market accounting requires the asset to be valued at what it would bring if sold in the market today. A big benefit for using this method is that the revenue normally generated throughout the life of a contract is instead realized immediately. If Enron entered into a twenty-year contract, the anticipated revenue over the entire contract was recognized in the first year. That also meant that the actual revenue generated annually on the deal was significantly smaller than the revenue reported on its balance sheets. Another problem was that the revenue started at zero each year, which meant that to show an increase, more and more contracts had to be signed every year.

Enron wanted to encourage out-of-the-box thinking and offered lucrative compensation plans that were tied directly to shareholder value; which included a base salary, and both annual and long-term incentives. The long-term incentive program issued nonqualified stock options and restrictive stock that vested over a period of time.

THE SKY IS THE LIMIT

Around this time there was a real push around the world to deregulate energy. In 1992, India began looking for foreign investors to help meet demand for electrical power in their country. On June 20, 1992, Enron signed a memorandum of understanding (MOU) with the Maharashtra State Electricity Board to build a power plant for the Dabhol Power Company. The $2.9 billion project was to be the cornerstone of Enron's international expansion. Construction began in 1996. By then, Enron had started its electricity trading operations and formed Enron Global Power and Pipelines to bid on energy projects in other developing countries.

In 1995, Enron opened its trading center in London, England. That led to their acquisition of Wessex Water, P.L.C., a major water company in the United Kingdom, and the formation of Azurix Corporation, a subsidiary of Enron.

In July 1997, Enron acquired Portland General Electric (PGE), a utility company in Portland, Oregon. In 1998, Enron invested $10 million in Rhythms NetConnections, Inc., an internet service provider. In 1999, Enron absorbed FirstPoint, a subsidiary of PGE that was developing a fiber optic network, and formed Enron Communications later renamed Enron Broadband Services and EnronOnline.

Enron was booming. The 1999 annual report said, "In 1999 we witnessed an acceleration of Enron's staggering pace of commercial innovation . . .revenue increased 28 percent to $40 billion, and net income before non-recurring items increased 37 percent to reach $957 million. Our total return to shareholders of 58 percent was eight times higher than our peer group and almost triple the S&P 500 return."[1]

BEHIND THE CURTAIN

It seemed there was no stopping Enron. Jeffrey Skilling and Kenneth Lay had their fingers on the pulse of the market and investors were happy. Underneath the glossy exterior lay a complex web of transactions meant to hide the reality that Enron wasn't making as much money as it was leading everyone to believe it was.

Enron had taken on a significant amount of debt and pressure was mounting. Wall Street had come to

---

1 Material taken from source (Enron Annual Report 1999, 2).

expect double-digit returns on investments and demanded that Enron show continued growth. Enron needed fresh capital to pursue new and greater projects to show that continued growth. Unfortunately the assets Enron had on its balance sheet were causing a problem. Large power-plant deals were not expected to generate any significant return on investment for many years.

Something had to be done to show profitability. Enron's business model had become heavily dependent upon credit for their trading operations. If Enron failed to qualify for an investment-grade credit rating, it would no longer have access to low-cost financing. Without that, Enron would not be able to continue its trading operations.

Enron had to find a way to take debt out of its balance sheet and show incoming revenue. It was decided that Enron would bundle the debt and sell it to outside investors. This would allow Enron to realize the cash flow it needed and dump the assets associated with the debt. In 1993, the Joint Energy Development Investments Limited Partnership (JEDI) was formed with Enron and the California Public Retirement System (CalPERS), each owning a fifty percent interest. JEDI was considered a nonconsolidated special-purpose entity (SPE).

The main attraction to creating a nonconsolidated entity was that the assets and liabilities transferred to the SPE would be completely removed from Enron's balance sheet. In contrast, a consolidated SPE is treated as a subsidiary with its assets and debts remaining on Enron's financial statements. There is an important accounting rule required for an entity to be considered nonconsolidated: it must have three percent of outside equity considered *fully at-risk* invested in the deal.

BENDING THE RULES

In 1997, CalPERS wanted to cash out of its investment. Their initial $250 million investment was now worth $383 million. Unfortunately, Enron wasn't able to secure another outside investor willing to invest in JEDI. If no investor could be found, JEDI would no longer be an SPE and Enron would have to transfer JEDI onto Enron's balance sheet. If this happened, the end-of-year earnings statement would be negatively affected.

A key contributor to the eventual demise of Enron was Andrew Fastow; who at this time was a senior vice president in the finance department. In 1998, he was promoted to Chief Financial Officer (CFO). Fastow presented a solution to Skilling: create a special-purpose entity that would assume CalPERS' position in the investment, and guarantee it with Enron stock. Skilling approved.

On November 5, 1997, Fastow presented to the Board a proposed sale of CalPERS interest in JEDI. He asked the Board to approve a corporate guarantee for two loans, a $383 million bridge loan and a $250 million loan to Chewco to secure the deal. That corporate guarantee of $383 million took away any unconsolidated status. There is no outside equity at-risk if Enron was guaranteeing the entire deal.

The specifics of the deal were:
- a $250 million loan, guaranteed by Enron
- a $132 million advance from JEDI
- an $11.4 million loan which included a $6.58 million advance by JEDI.

The $11.4 million loan was the required three percent outside equity meant to qualify JEDI as a nonconsolidated entity. Enron employee Michael Kopper, a subordinate of Fastow, created two additional SPEs and personally invested $125,000 total into both entities. The bank funding the loan to Kopper required a reserve account be opened for $6.58 million to further guarantee the $11.4 million loan, which was also paid for by JEDI.

GOING WITH THE CROWD

The deal was as complicated as it sounds, and anyone without a finance background, including the Board that was comprised of competent and educated individuals, could likely become confused. I imagine there was a lot of pressure to approve the transaction with the end of the year only eight weeks away. They might have trusted that Fastow, a senior employee of Enron, would never intentionally propose a deal that went against any accounting regulations. They also might have assumed that Arthur Andersen, the highly respected accounting firm overseeing this deal, would not have helped construct a deal that was unethical.

Arthur Andersen also signed off on this deal. They had the requisite financial background, but also charged Enron a consulting fee for their participation in evaluating these deals. The more complicated the deal, the more money they could charge. Or, one could argue, were they also confused by the transactions but because they were financial specialists didn't want to risk questioning them and seeming incompetent?

Kenneth Lay, Chief Executive Officer (CEO) of Enron, arrived at the meeting during Fastow's presentation. Possibly he missed out on crucial information that might have made him question the deal. I am sure there was a high level of trust in Jeffrey Skilling, the Chief Operating Officer (COO) of Enron, as he was in charge of overseeing the day-to-day operations.

ONE LIE LEADS TO ANOTHER LIE

In 1999, Enron began losing money on its investments, which threatened to bring down Enron's annual earnings. Enron needed to find a way to boost earnings before the end of the year. Fastow offered up another solution. He would create another SPE, named LJM2, that would buy those poorly performing assets from Enron, no questions asked. In return, Enron would agree to guarantee the investors of LJM2 against any losses.

The Board had already approved Fastow's involvement in another SPE called LJM, which was used to hedge Enron's investment in Rhythms, a business providing broadband Internet access to large enterprises and tele-communications carriers. When he brought LJM2 before the Board he asked them to approve his direct involvement as manager of the SPE, a violation of the Enron code-of-ethics. Board approval was required before Fastow could assume that managerial role and retain his position of CFO at Enron.

This serious conflict of interest was justified because Enron stood to gain more with Fastow driving the train than with anybody else. At least this is what the Board was told. Enron would be able to engage in transactions that blurred the legal lines. His familiarity with both sides of the deal would allow it to progress at lightning speed for a fraction of the cost. The Board was assured that stringent rules regarding review and approval were in place.

The reality was that those controls were all talk and no action. Those in charge failed to be as diligent in their responsibilities as they should have been. The annual audit and review to be conducted by the Compensation Committee was a formality and never questioned the material provided. The Board may have assumed since they weren't hearing any negative reports, all was well.

TRYING TO SAVE ENRON

It wasn't until after Skilling abruptly stepped down from his post as CEO of Enron on August 14, 2001, a mere six months after being appointed to the position, that Lay fully realized the precarious situation Enron was in. Enormous amounts of debt had been hidden away in countless SPEs created by Fastow and his team. The lethal trap was laid deep within the web of legal and accounting language. The cold truth was these SPEs all had triggers which allowed the outside investors to demand immediate payment by Enron if its stock price slipped or its credit rating was downgraded.

Faced with the decision to either continue to hide the debt and postpone the inevitable, or unravel the SPEs and face the consequences; Lay chose the latter. According to his federal indictment, after he took over as CEO, Lay was informed of the severe financial and operational problems threatening Enron's existence. As he investigated options, such as mergers and restructuring, Lay continued to reassure the public, its investors, and employees, that all was well.

The media had started reporting on discrepancies found in Enron financial statements and many employees had grown concerned. On September 26, 2001, Lay held an online meeting with Enron employees and stated, "The company is fundamentally sound. The balance sheet is strong. Our financial liquidity has never been stronger . . . My personal belief is that Enron stock is an incredible bargain at current prices and we will look back a couple of years from now and see the great opportunity that we currently have." After hearing this powerful statement, many employees reportedly rushed out and bought more of Enron's stock.[2]

WATCHING ENRON FALL

On October 23, 2001, at another employee meeting, Lay attempted to quell concerns after reporting a $1.2 billion reduction in shareholder equity on the third-quarter earnings release. "Our liquidity is fine. As a matter of fact, it's better than fine, it's strong. . . as sad as the current market price is--and I've certainly lost a substantial portion of my net worth and my family's net worth. . .But I also know that many of you who were a lot wealthier six to nine months ago are now concerned about the college education for your kids, maybe the mortgage on your house, maybe your retirement. . .But we're going to get it back."[3]

During this time Enron went forward with its plan to

2 United States District Court, Southern District of Texas, Houston Division, *U.S. Securities and Exchange Commission vs. Kenneth R. Lay,* et al, Civil Action No. H-04-0284 (Harmon), Second Amended Complaint, July 2004, Page 36.

3 United States District Court, Southern District of Texas, Houston Division, *U.S. Securities and Exchange Commission vs. Kenneth R. Lay,* et al, Civil Action No. H-04-0284 (Harmon), Second Amended Complaint, July 2004, Page 36.

change the administrators of the Enron Corporation Savings Plan. Employees would have to complete any trade requests before 3:00 p.m. on Friday, October 26, or else wait until the blackout period was scheduled to end on November 19. On October 26 the closing price for Enron stock was $15.40.

A few days after the blackout started, Enron's Benefits Department asked if the blackout period could be suspended or accelerated. Because the transition of records had already begun the best option was to try to end it as quickly as possible. Enron requested a postcard be mailed to all participants in the plan advising them that the end date of the blackout period was being moved up and urged them to monitor the Enron website for up-to-date information. Sadly, when the blackout was lifted on November 13, many employees saw the stock as a bargain and invested more instead of selling.

On November 9, Enron announced it was merging with its competitor Dynegy, Inc. The $9.5 billion deal hinged on Enron's credit rating. If the rating were to fall below investment grade, also known as junk status, the deal would be terminated. Dynegy's market share in its trading department alone would increase from six percent to about twenty-three percent. The stakes for both sides were high.

When markets opened on November 13, the stock was trading at $9.50. The stock continued to hold for a few days but began a more serious decline after November 20. On November 28, Enron's credit was downgraded to junk bond status and a few hours later Dynegy announced it was backing out of the merger. Trading on Enron's stock was halted just after noon at a price of 61 cents.

The loss devastated Enron employees who had invested heavily in Enron stock. In January 2001, the corporate savings plan and employee stock ownership plan contained over $2.1 billion in Enron stock, which accounted for two-thirds of the total assets within those plans. In December that value had dropped to approximately $10 million. On December 2, Enron filed for bankruptcy.

A NEW BEGINNING

For everyone who left Enron on December 3, it marked a significant day in their life. The reality was that there is more to this story than just those 4,000 people and it extends further than Houston; it encompassed the world. Families as far away as Australia, India, and England and as close as Oregon, California and Illinois had to find a new path.

Not everyone lost their entire retirement, but they all suffered in one way or another. This book delves beyond the headlines and asks those pointed questions of those most vulnerable, those most like you and me. Their stories are anything but ordinary, but their ability to rise above and find a new way is what makes each one memorable.

"Adversity is the state in which man most easily becomes acquainted with himself, being especially free of admirers then."

-John Wooden

JAMES BUCKNER

OFFSITE LOCATION IN HOUSTON, TEXAS
1 YEAR 9 MONTHS

*I*t was early 2000 when Buckner was approached by Enron to work as a field engineer for Enron Broadband Services (EBS). "I talked to a few people at Enron and everybody was real nice; a really good bunch. They talked about some intriguing concepts, such as bandwidth trading, and I thought, 'Let's see what this is about.'"

As he was waiting in the lobby for his interview, Buckner was struck by the abnormally positive attitude shared by everyone who worked there. "I remember sitting in the lobby and I see a lot of people and for the first time in my life, I see a lot of people actually excited going to work. Now this is a place to work!"

Buckner's office was at the Interstate 45 North, Greenspoint Mall area in an old shopping center near Houston, specifically designed for telecommunications carriers, known in the industry as a telecom hotel. It didn't take long before he noticed a few red flags. "The longer I was around there, I noticed there was something a little odd going on. It was one of those things that you can't put your finger on, but it's kind of like the old phrase, 'If you don't understand it, there is something funny going on.'"

SEEING A PROBLEM

In the summer of 2000, Buckner noticed that Enron was selling fiber ribbons to a company he had never heard of, LJM. Because the individual fibers in a fiber optic cable are extremely delicate, ribbons are used to ensure stability and durability. Not all the ribbons within the cable are used by the same company. In the telecommunications industry it is common for companies to buy, lease, or swap ribbons from one another.

He looked into LJM but was not able to find anything about it, so he let it go. After the bankruptcy it was revealed that LJM was a special-purpose entity created by the Enron CFO, Andrew Fastow, to artificially inflate Enron's yearly earnings. LJM would purchase Enron's poorly-performing assets for a set period of time with a guarantee from Enron to either find another buyer or buy the asset back.

In early 2001, Buckner began to question how Enron was making any money. "I noticed we only had a couple of telecom customers, and I thought, 'What are we actually doing here?'"

He noticed that EBS was purchasing more equipment without the customer base to justify the expenditure. "I just didn't see what was going on. It was almost like they were trying to build a redundant system when, in fact, if you are trying to build a redundant system, the first thing you do is pick a different backbone cable. . .You don't have two redundant systems in the same cable; it just doesn't work, because if you have a cable cut you knock out both systems. I was thinking, 'What is going on here?'"

SEEING THE SIGNS

Buckner finally found his answers in the most unlikely way. "I don't know why I was home that day and had the TV on CNBC, but I think there was a reason for it. The host of the show, Ron Insana, asked his guest a very pointed question: 'Is Enron headed for bankruptcy?' I thought, 'Now, wait a minute!' But I listened for a little bit and the guest made a pretty compelling case, and over time I started seeing some signs that made me think, 'Oh, this is going to hurt!'"

When the second-quarter earnings were released on July 12, 2001, they painted a bleak picture for EBS. The press release read, "Enron Broadband Services reported a $102 million IBIT (Income Before Interest and Taxes) loss for the second quarter. . .This quarter's loss reflects significantly lower revenues and comparable operating expenses from a year ago. Enron expects to significantly modify the cost structure of its broadband business in the near term to reduce future losses associated with a lower revenue outlook."

At the moment Buckner began to consider the possibility of unemployment. The only thing he could think of to do was to save as much money as he could. "I reviewed my take-home pay and I did a monthly budget. I realized I could save up to $1000 a paycheck. I cut back on a few things and I really watched the expenses like a hawk. I cut back on the cable TV and kept the Internet and the phone, because there were certain things you had to keep."

On October 16, 2001, Enron released their third-quarter earnings report. Its third paragraph confirmed Buckner's worst fears: "Non-recurring charges totaling $1.01 billion after-tax, or $(1.11) loss per diluted share, were recognized for the third quarter of 2001."

THE DEATH OF ENRON

Shortly thereafter, Buckner noticed a significant change in the atmosphere at Enron. "Then I saw from the inside as to what happened. . .by October 2001, whatever happiness I remember seeing there was gone. The entire mood had changed. And even though I was twenty miles from the epicenter, you could almost sense it."

Around Thanksgiving, Buckner and two co-workers began to fear that the next day would be their last on the job. "We started talking: 'Look, guys, it's coming, we just don't know when.' We started taking our stuff home so when the time came we could just leave quickly."

The air was thick with anticipation when Buckner went into work on December 3. "When we walked in there, we got in around 8:00 a.m.; we knew about it, we were just thinking, 'What happens now?' I read about it on the Drudge Report and heard about it in the local news media as well. . . At about 10:30 we started getting phone calls. . . 'Hey, guys, we lost our jobs and. . .it's been nice working with you.'"

It was a day none of them would ever forget. "We knew that at the end of Monday that roughly 4,000 people lost their jobs; we had the TV on, just watching what happened. Remote access had been shut down and we couldn't even access our company email that day. It was like somebody flipped the switch. My manager had to fly to Los Angeles and a few other places and he was firing people. We left one person in L.A., Dallas and Chicago."

They continued to come into work as they had before; Buckner and his peers waited for their time to come. "We had not seen our manager for a couple of days. By Thursday afternoon we had resigned ourselves to the fact that Friday was going to be our last day. We all decided to go ahead and since we have been working as a team for so long, we would end it as a team. So on December 7 of 2001, which was ironically the sixtieth anniversary of Pearl Harbor, at 9:00 a.m. we walked into our office area. Our manager was sitting there and he basically said, "'Well, that's it; you're fired.' We handed over our badges and walked out the front door—together."

Buckner knew he needed to get out of town and collect his thoughts. "I went to my place, picked up some clothes for the weekend, made a phone call to my dad, and let him know I was coming. By lunchtime I was in a small town outside of San Antonio talking with my dad, watching some news, and reading about what happened in Houston."

ENDURING UNEMPLOYMENT

He took a few days to gather his thoughts before returning to Houston. "I tried to line up some interviews, and it was rough adjusting to unemployment. You are used to getting up and one day you get up and you are not going to work. After a couple of days your body doesn't know what is going on. You want to go to work but there is no place for you to go to. I was unemployed from December 7 until April 22."

Buckner posted his résumé online and called around to people he knew, but it was taking longer than he anticipated. "I had one interview with a company in Houston that happened right in December. Unfortunately I did not get the job because they thought I was a little overqualified. A few other things came up, but they weren't in my field. I went to a job interview at a local car dealership but realized it was not for me."

He felt fortunate to have the savings he built up the previous year. "I still had money, I wasn't desperate for work, and I was at a point where I could still wait it out. I figured I still had funds until May or June if I stretched it. Around the first part of April 2002, one of my old bosses at Enron calls me up and says, 'James, would you like to work for me?' I said, 'Sure!'"

The long road of unemployment was over and Buckner found himself back in the telecommunications business. "It was a field position. I had a company vehicle—that really helped me out. I got to see a lot of the country and I worked with a couple of people I am still friends with to this day. I looked at myself as a survivor."

THE FINANCIAL IMPACT

When the dust settled at the end of 2001, Buckner's retirement account was in the black. "When I joined up with Enron, I heard of people sticking a lot of their retirement into Enron stock. I have always been a student of diversification when necessary. . .I had a weird feeling that there were people counting on this money for their retirement. And I was thinking, 'Are you sure you want to put all your money in there?'"

When he sat down to determine where to put his retirement funds, he looked beyond the hype surrounding the Enron stock and chose a more conservative investment approach. "I put in just five percent, just a token amount.

I researched my investments, I did what I could; we had some very good mutual funds in the company. Three of those investment choices made so much money that I was able not only to overcome my losses in the Enron stock fund, but I actually came out about $4,000 ahead."

When the Enron stock started to lose value significantly, Buckner was blocked from selling off his Enron stock until about two weeks before it crashed. To this day he finds the timing of the administrative change to the retirement account to be suspicious. "I lost about $3,000 in Enron stock. The 401(k) lockdown that we had, that was another fishy thing. . .If their own employees smelled blood in the water, they would sell their stock and tell their friends to sell their stock. I think it was more along the lines of trying to hold in all the suckers as long as they could. About two weeks before, once they lifted restriction, I tried to move as much money as I could, even though I ate some losses. . .I think that action saved me a little bit of money."

A NEW APPRECIATION

Before this time, Buckner had always enjoyed a comfortable life. "Now I knew what it was like to be poor and without a job. When it hits you like that, you undergo an intense self-examination; you wonder, 'Why did this happen?' In my case it amounted to, 'All right, this is happening for a reason, and I just have to get through it.'"

He sees his lengthy unemployment as a blessing. "I have always believed that God is always in control and He is not going to give you anything more than you can handle. This was probably one of the best moments in my life because I was able to examine myself and learn a few things."

Buckner used the extra time to grow as a person and cultivate his relationship with his parents. "I actually got to spend time with my mom and dad. Gas was only about a dollar a gallon; it wasn't that hard to go down and stay with my dad or mom for a few days. I would work on the farm, do stuff basically; I was always keeping myself busy. I learned the value of hard work. I developed a really good work ethic and it was one of those things where you realize that sometimes you just have to be careful and you just have to trust you are making the right decisions."

While he understands the difficulties faced by many, he believes there is no excuse for failing to take the simple necessary steps to protect one's financial future. "After Enron, I became a little more understanding; I became a little more compassionate when I remember the people who lost their money. . .Today, I see people who don't even make the basic financial decisions. . .I am talking about your average worker who hasn't taken the time to study or understand what they are getting into. That is where I do not have compassion and understanding."

Buckner believes it was necessary for him to leave his previous job and work for Enron in order to be able to find his calling. "When the company we were doing the work for filed for bankruptcy in July 2003, I thought, 'Oh my, here we go again. I don't need to go through this again.' The moment I heard about that bankruptcy filing, I started hitting the pavement. In a strange sense of irony I went back to my old employer [pre-Enron]. They offered me a job with a bit better pay and better manager, and I was able to pull the escape handle and get out of a rough situation. That is how I was able to find my calling."

Now, he never has to work another day in his life. "I found out after of all this that I had been through life not knowing what my goals were, and I realized I needed to find my calling. . .If you are lucky enough to find your calling, you never have to work another day in your life. That is what I do. I don't work at my job. I help people get connected to the Internet all over the world, help people connect with their families, especially those on boats, ships, and very remote areas. I feel that I have a very rewarding job, even though I don't get to see the people I help. I know that the work I do makes a difference in the lives of thousands of people all over the world. That is what I consider my calling."

WHO IS REALLY GUILTY?

The day Kenneth Lay was found guilty remains clear in Buckner's mind. "I saw the picture before the judgment and I saw the picture afterwards, and I could see that he lost his will to live. . .a man who was spending everything for five or six years to salvage the one thing he couldn't buy. . .his reputation. . .therefore he had nothing else to live for."

Buckner firmly believes the verdict was correct but contends the real perpetrators escaped prosecution. "He was complicit in the actions of the company; he was the head of that company, and as far as I am concerned, yes, he was guilty. . .but the real criminals are the bankers and the investment houses that let this happen, and unfortunately they are still the same ones causing the same problems we see today."

He believes crises will continue to plague America unless those directly responsible are reined in. "I am ten years older and a lot more wiser than my days at Enron, but it pains me to see what was going on with mortgage market. . .

I know that I am going to see it play out again. If you realize that life goes in ten- or twenty-year cycles, I think the older you get, the more you see things repeat themselves whether you like it or not. Life always goes on in cycles."

A WORD OF ADVICE

Stay informed to see the signs ahead of time. "I have a Google news alert to email me when an article comes up. I don't really read the mainstream media too much except for Drudge, but I do look at stuff overseas—*The Guardian* in the U.K., for example. I read *The Wall Street Journal*, Bloomberg, and a couple of financial blogs: Market Ticker and Zero Hedge. I am always looking for the signs that tell me what's coming. To me nothing happens by accident; you should always be able to see the signs."

You are in control of your future. "If you apply yourself and you go ahead and find something that you like to do and something that's rewarding, life will get better; it does get better. This is the greatest country in the whole entire world. You have every opportunity, so get off your butt and make a life for yourselves. It is up to you to make your own way. You can't assume anything in this world; the days of company loyalty have been gone since the 1980s. Now you have to look within yourself. We are in a knowledge-based economy now, and it's what you know, how you can disseminate it, and how you can monetize it. And that's where we are today."

Thoroughly investigate companies before getting hired. "I have really researched companies now, on Yahoo.com, they have a load of information. . .I look at the insider buying and selling ratios. That is one of the things I look at when I look at a public company. I want to see what the insiders are doing."

Be cautious of companies with a lot of insider selling. "What I like to see is a company where the insiders are buying stock. To me they know something is going on, otherwise why would they buy the stock? Conversely, I would avoid a company where you have insiders engaged in a big pattern of selling."

FOR THOSE FACING A LAYOFF

The future is bright but requires action. "It can get better; it does get better, but you have to apply yourself."

Save as much as possible. "I saw what was coming; I did what I could to prepare. If I save this money now, it will get me through this rough patch."

Take some time to regroup before looking for that next job. "When the layoff does happen, don't try to set up something right away. You need to have some time, don't take too much time, but take some time to get away and refocus."

Stay busy every day. "On days you aren't job searching, if you have a friend who has a job and needs some help, go ahead and see if they can use you. At least it will get you out of the house. You have to keep yourself busy. Employers can tell if you haven't been doing anything or if you have actually been working at something. Volunteer, do something, have a reason to get up every morning. . .If you want to take the time to get some education, take classes, and find something that you want to do."

" It can be liberating to get fired because you realize the world doesn't end. There's other ways to make money, better jobs."

-Ron Livingston

BRIAN FRITZ

PORTLAND, OREGON – 18 YEARS

*B*rian Fritz had been working for Portland General Electric (PGE) since 1983. He became an employee of Enron when it acquired PGE in 1997. "Initially, the fiber optic business was under PGE as FirstPoint. Later we went through various different names, but we ended up as Enron Broadband and were headquartered in Portland."

For the first time in his career, Fritz experienced total flexibility within his normal rigid environment. "Within the Broadband business unit all employees were given freedom of responsibility and empowerment. You were hired to do a job, you were expected to do that job and you went and did it. If you didn't do that job, then you had the choice go find another job and in many cases people were asked to do just that. Which was great. It was more of a free-enterprise-type company rather than a regulated company."

He had few internal rules to follow. All Enron expected in return was results. "PGE was a regulated company in Oregon. To me, a change from the regulated world to Broadband was great. I could go do what I knew how to do and was given all the tools I needed to go do that job, was expected to go do it, and keep senior management apprised of what I was doing, but basically told to go do it."

With state after state deregulating, Enron needed someone who was knowledgeable enough about the industry to be able to accurately assess the viability of a project. "I spent quite a bit of time working in Houston, going through proposal documents and doing a lot of reviews and a lot of work to help them get bid documents together and how to appraise bid documents from vendors on equipment, and doing a lot of due diligence. . .They didn't have anyone that knew anything about power plants to actually go and walk through them and then write a report about what kind of shape they were in, were they maintained well, et cetera. I did a lot of that work."

ADJUSTING TO THE ENRON CULTURE

The environment at PGE, albeit bureaucratic, was very friendly and Fritz had earned a lot of respect from his co-workers over the many years he had worked there. After he started working for Enron, that mutual respect was discarded and he was wanted only as long as he was deemed pertinent to the task at hand. "They sucked out your knowledge and once they didn't need you, you were done. . .It was very competitive. I think those people who were developing those sites, they made a lot of money being the developer and they didn't want to share it with anybody, obviously. But they definitely would use your knowledge to further their plan."

Fritz and his team were constantly defending their projects against hostile takeover attempts by rogue teams in Houston. "Even though we were the ones that developed the business, got the business going, got the infrastructure built, we were still viewed as the outsider. We would be working along and all of a sudden we would start getting memos, phone calls, emails from people and groups that we didn't even know who they were that would just insert themselves in the process and try and take control of it."

The audacity of their co-workers was such a culture shock to the Portland team that it didn't take long for relations to sour. "It was annoying, for more than one reason. One, obviously anybody who managing a program or a project doesn't want people coming in and trying to take control; two, they didn't know anything about the business. So they would try to come in and take control and push an agenda that didn't make sense."

Fritz was part of the team that developed Points of Presence (POP) for fiber. These POPs were specific locations where fibers from different locations came together. POPs are located in big cities with a large amount of equipment that is used to manage the signals on those fibers. One day Fritz's manager received an email from a senior executive in Houston. "He sent a report out to all the Senior Managers with a list of all these POP sites and said that these were all done."

Fritz's manager was immediately alarmed as he knew Fritz was managing those POP sites and nothing had been said about them being finished. Fritz's manager immediately contacted Fritz and asked if the POP sites listed on the report were indeed completed. Fritz was taken aback. "I said, 'What are you talking about? Many of these were not done; in fact some hadn't even begun!'"

Fritz's manager went back and wrote a heated email to the author of the report. "He basically asked, 'What are you talking about, are you smoking crack?'. . .He had to apologize later, but that was the type of B.S. that would happen. We found out that [the author of the report], was a lead over a group of people that basically self-formed and said, 'We are going to start tracking this stuff and getting it done,' without any knowledge of where they were, what they were, and how to complete them."

SEEING A PROBLEM

Fritz was working for Enron Broadband Services as a Senior Project Manager in 2001. "One of my responsibilities was to review all contracts with other companies and put a technical eye to it, so to speak. The way it worked is we would go build a fiber route between two or more major cities, but we would put more fiber in the ground than what we needed for the Broadband business, and you would turn around and sell or trade the excess fiber to other communications companies."

Fritz noticed something he had never seen before. "I reviewed all those contracts and a contract came across my desk one day where Broadband was selling most, if not all of the owned and in-process-of-being-acquired fiber to a company called LJM2."

LJM2 was another entity created by Andrew Fastow, CFO of Enron. It was immediately apparent to Fritz that something about this wasn't right. "As I reviewed the contract I thought, 'Now, wait a minute, I know probably about ninety percent of players of the industry and this wasn't one of them.'"

Fritz and his co-worker attempted to find out where this company came from and who owned it, but nothing could be found. "So we flagged the contract and we started asking questions up the Broadband management chain and were told to stop asking questions and approve the transaction. We knew something was up, something was not right and we pushed back on our management a little bit and were told in no uncertain terms, 'Leave it and approve it.' We had been told from the highest to leave this alone. After that was when the red flags went up for the other guy and me reviewing the contract. We knew something was wrong; we just did not know what, or the extent."

As the year wore on, Fritz watched as those around him were laid off. He knew it was only a matter of time before he too was gone. He and those who remained could only watch and wait for their time to come. "We weren't the first wave to be laid off. We had already seen at least two other groups get laid off. You could feel it coming: The stock price was dropping, work was slowing down; we were told to quit spending money. You knew it was coming; it was just a matter of time. Those of us who were left would come into work and talk about the future, or lack of, at Broadband, 'Well, when do you think it will happen?'"

As the walls were coming down around them, everyone believed that the layoffs were only temporary. "Nobody thought that the company was going to end up where it did in full bankruptcy and completely out of business. Everyone we talked to would say, 'Yes, we will get laid off, but Enron will come back and there will be jobs again.'"

GOODBYE, ENRON

In August of 2001, Fritz was laid off. Even though he had seen it happen to others, it still left him shaken. "The worst part was when you get the layoff notification and you are looking around the office and everyone is getting the same message. Because even though you know it is coming, it is the finality. You are hurt; you are at a loss, wondering, 'What are we going to do?'"

To ease the pain of being laid off, Enron offered a very generous severance package. "I basically walked away with a year's pay. I didn't get all of that because of the way it was set up. I got half of it up front and the remainder over the following six months. It was like you were getting paid. But of course, when they started heading for bankruptcy, all those programs were cut off."

Even after being laid off, Enron was still looking after them. "The company brought in people to provide training on developing résumés, how to interview, where to look for a job, how to look for a job. Then you were allowed to use your office, the resources in the office, to help put together your résumé, start making contacts and begin the process of finding a new job. They even brought in a grief counselor to work with you, tell you how you are going to feel because you lost your job, and how you could work through those feelings."

Fritz knows he was one of the last to receive this level of generosity. "I was friends with [an Enron Director] and she said we were pretty lucky, because the next round of layoffs were going to be, 'Two weeks' pay; goodbye.' She knew what the program was going to do. She didn't know there were going to be more layoffs; she just knew that the round of layoffs that I was in, that was the last of the generous severance package. My guess for discontinuation was that the company figured out the program was not sustainable."

FACING THE FINANCIAL IMPACT

When Enron purchased PGE, they offered incentives to roll over employees' 401(k) s into Enron stock. Brian Fritz remembers, "Some PGE employees put their entire 401(k) in Enron stock. We were given that option. I wouldn't say I was a savvy investor, but I know better than that, unless you were to do that and closely follow the market then change your percentages as the market fluctuated."

It was not an easy task to simply accept Enron stock and then cash out. "You were limited on the changes you could make in your 401(k), and towards the end, the system was locked and not many changes could be made. . .So at that point, once that conversion was made, you rode out the market. In my case, I had Enron stock options, plus Enron stock in my 401(k) as part of the company matching program; I had enough stock in the company. There were always all kinds of deals to increase the amount of company stock you owned; I thought it was another way to get hooked into buying more stock."

At one point, Brian Fritz's co-worker warned him to sell out. "The stock market was his hobby and he started doing some research and he warned some of us in the department, 'This is going to collapse.' He said, 'Their earnings are too low for their price value. This can't be sustained.' He sold off every option he could and converted all he could in his 401(k) account. He warned us to do the same."

Fritz was counting on the stock to contribute to his future. He was 46 and looking forward to retiring comfortably. He felt he had the luxury of time to ride out the highs and lows of the market. Based on internal communication, he discounted his co-worker's advice. "When you have senior management telling you everything is okay, everything is great, things are going well, you start to buy in; you start to believe. You want to believe."

He decided to take the gamble and ended up losing most of his retirement funds. "I lost, based on the high mark of their stock price, about a million and a half."

Fritz has little to say about the loss. "That is life and that is the way it goes. It is up to the individual to take in the information and make the decision; you cannot place the blame or responsibility elsewhere."

While this loss was initially overwhelming, Fritz learned some hard lessons. "I did two things wrong: I didn't put a stop loss on my stock options; that, I had control over. And when I got laid off, I had the option of taking my 401(k) out of Enron and investing it myself, rolling it over into a tax-sheltered investment. But I hesitated and the stock price went to zero. So the stock crash affected my options and my 401(k). The loss is my own fault; I could have cashed out. I had my hand on the brass ring and someone spilled some oil on it and I slipped. I should have known better; the signs were there. I just didn't want to believe it, and didn't think it would hit rock bottom like it did. Back then, you didn't see a Fortune 500 company just come apart like that. It just didn't happen."

GOING BACK TO WORK FOR PGE

Life right after the layoff wasn't so bad for Fritz. "I was still getting paid, so I was on vacation. I didn't even look for a job immediately. There was stuff around the house I wanted to do. I didn't even look for a job, didn't even look hard probably until maybe February."

Through his contacts, Fritz was able to find work. "A guy that I had worked with at PGE asked me if I was interested in coming in and doing some contract work with him."

The opportunity seemed perfect. Fritz knew the environment, knew the job and knew everyone he would be working with. To his surprise, it turned out to be the longest six months of his life. "That was probably a worse experience than what I went through at Enron."

Many at PGE lost their retirement when Enron's stock fell. As a result, there was much animosity for those who had worked directly for Enron. When Fritz arrived at PGE, everyone knew he was an ex-Enron employee. "It was known, those of us that worked directly for Enron. People knew."

Those who personally knew Fritz treated him respectfully. "I knew some of the people from before, and generally I wouldn't get the harsh words, the bad vibes from them, because I knew them."

It was the ones who didn't know him that tended to assume the worst of him. Fritz remembers an especially contentious conversation with a female co-worker. She said, "Since I worked for Enron I must be a dirty S.O.B. also and part of the problem. I was part of the cause of why her 401(k) took such a hit. I looked at her and said, 'But you still have a job. I can look out the door and point you to ten people who you're better off than; be they homeless, without a job, or barely scraping by.'"

"She looked back at me and said, 'But you got paid way more than I did and you probably pocketed a bunch of money.'"

Fritz didn't know how to respond. She was merely voicing a general belief held by those who suffered. Working there wasn't worth it anymore; he knew it was time to go. "It was hard to get up in the morning knowing you were going to face this underlying hostility because you had worked for a company, and really for a company you had no control over. It was a company you worked for that was purchased and held on to. You had no control. But you were viewed as one of the bad guys."

A NEW WORKPLACE, A NEW MAN

Working for Enron had its benefits and it spoke volumes on Fritz's résumé. It was one of the reasons why he was chosen to be interviewed by his current employer. "They looked at the experience I had at Enron and looked favorably on that. They looked at the experience and not the company."

Without Enron, Fritz would have been a very different person. "When I worked at Portland General, it was the old-school utility where outside-the-box thinking was frowned on, to a certain extent: 'This is how we do business and we'll keep doing it that way.'"

Enron helped Fritz evolve as a person. "I think on the good side it gave me more confidence in my abilities in what I can do. It showed me that you can take control and you can use that freedom to go do what you are trained and know how to do."

It helped Fritz become a more effective manager, "I use that same philosophy of empowering people to do the job. They know how they can do it. Not micromanaging what they do. Let them make a mistake. It is not life or death. We'll survive the mistakes people make around here and we will learn from it."

Fritz knows in order to find the reward, one must be willing to take the risk. "On the other side of the coin, you tried something new. If it worked, that's great! There is always more than one way to get from Point A to Point B; we should be trying to learn new ways. I learned that while I worked at Enron."

Fritz uses his experience to change and empower others he comes in contact with. "It has helped me in my career as I have managed people. The feedback I have gotten from the different departments I have run, the different people that report to me, appreciate that. I think it is kind of scary at first because somebody isn't telling them how to get from A to B. Somebody is showing them, here is A and we've got to get to B; how are we going to do it? For some people that's kind of scary. Once they do it, though, my experience around here has been, they are grateful for being allowed to have control over their task and that is how they want to keep doing their jobs."

He also knows that employee freedom should be somewhere in the middle of both extremes to be truly successful. "At Portland General there was some freedom, but management had their finger on most everything that went on to the extent that the micromanagement hindered your ability to effectively perform your job. At Enron, until things went wrong, your managers didn't really know the day-to-day minutiae of your work, didn't track or follow what you were doing at that level. It was at a very high level. After you would finish something, 'Okay, now let's move on to the next one. Let me know when you're done.' In my current job there is more of a balance. I am allowed the freedom to do my job and given the responsibility required to do it without the micromanagement aspects."

A WORD OF ADVICE

Be aware of your surroundings. "Keep your eye on the signs. If you run into something that looks like a duck, smells like a duck, it is probably a duck. Keep your eyes open and look for those signs."

Don't believe everything you hear. "Regardless of what your senior managers are telling you, don't ignore what the experts say."

Get financial advice. "Do some due diligence when you are given something such as a stock option. Understand what are your rights, what can I do with these, talk to someone who knows investments and knows what you should be doing so you can protect yourself from a free fall where the stock fell so fast you didn't have a chance to do anything."

Don't invest heavily in one stock. "Diversify. Keep it diversified. That is how you protect yourself. So if one stock goes south, you have others to rely on."

Know what to do when you see a red flag. "When I got the message of 'This contract is good, pass it through,' now I would recognize that, 'Okay, something's drastically wrong and now it is time to protect myself.' In my case, in that instance, where I had the stock options, maybe I would have sold them all. I had more that weren't in my control yet, that hadn't come to term, but I had a lot that were within my control, and so sell them; get what you can now.

Maybe your red flag disappears and nothing happens, but maybe it doesn't. If you have a chance, you have other stock in that company and got a chance to get it out, get it out. That's what I would have done differently. Knowing now what happened, it is easy to say what I could have done, but bottom line is it's the individual's responsibility. You have to watch out for yourself."

FOR THOSE FACING A LAYOFF

Talk to a counselor. "Find someone who can explain and walk you through the emotional stages that you are going to go through with a layoff."

Take some time to regroup. "You need to process it; you aren't going to suppress those feelings."

Take steps now to protect yourself financially. "I was more angry at myself for not seeing it coming, and not doing something to protect myself and my investment and the investment for my family."

Keep a positive perspective and don't take it personally. "I am not bitter about it. Really, it was a good experience. I learned a lot; I learned a lot about myself. It really helped me grow as a person. Yes, there's the downsides, which there always are with losing a job, but that's part of life. Nobody's protected; anybody can lose a job tomorrow, because your company goes under or it is determined you are not needed anymore, for whatever reason."

"All changes, even the most longed for, have their melancholy; for what we leave behind us is a part of ourselves; we must die to one life before we can enter another."

-Anatole France

KENTON ERWIN

PORTLAND, OREGON – 6 YEARS

*I*t was the summer of 1997 when Kenton Erwin found out his company was being bought out and his job was in jeopardy. "I had been working with a company that was in some of the same lines of business that Enron was in, also in Houston. It was sold to a smaller company that didn't have the appetite for keeping everything that they had acquired. They laid off about two-thirds of the people."

He felt very fortunate to have landed a position at Enron right before he was to be laid off. "I could see the writing on the wall for that, and there didn't seem to be space for me at the new company, and that's when I started looking around and found Enron. It was just lucky timing and I happened to get lucky during the interview process."

ONE OF MANY

Erwin worked in the legal department for Enron Capital and Trade Resources, a subsidiary of Enron. It was amazing to him how large that department was in comparison to what he was used to. "A pretty big company might have maybe twenty lawyers in-house, but here we had 150 and company-wide there were about 250 lawyers; that kind of blew my mind. But one reason that you needed so many lawyers at Enron was because so much of what they were doing was complex, the first of its kind."

Enron prided itself on being innovative and on the cutting-edge of technology. Those ideas didn't always pass the test when sent through the legal department. The problem was, Enron never wanted to hear "no," so the attorneys were assigned the difficult task of making it work but remaining within the confines of the law. "That's why it was so great to work there. Clients would walk in with these ideas and they had to be so creative to think this stuff up and sometimes it wasn't practical. . .but a lot of times it was just brilliant. And complicated deals take a lot of lawyering, and they were always complicated."

It soon became apparent that Enron was taking extensive measures to keep debt off its balance sheet. "One of the reasons, we learned over time, that it was complicated is because Enron didn't want to put a lot of debt on its balance sheet. Had I been an accountant I might have viewed that as a warning sign. Later I met a couple of people who started saying it was a warning sign, but at the time it just made the deals more complicated to do."

Enron created a culture that fostered innovation and they were constantly encouraging their employees to think differently. "Enron wanted you to think outside the box, you know—no limits, and those lessons are good ones for anybody, although it's yin-yang. In any organization you've got to foster a spirit of innovation and entrepreneurial-ism, but also have enough people who can either make it happen or see issues that could be a problem, and figure out ways to avoid the problems even while you are trying to do new things and forge ahead. Enron probably didn't have enough of that balance. They were probably a little too far on the innovation side and not quite strong enough on the caution and make-it-right side."

MOVING TO PORTLAND

Erwin and his family wanted to move out of Houston at some time. Enron provided the opportunity to change positions and move to Portland, Oregon to work for a new upstart called Enron Broadband. "What they were doing was slowly and methodically trying to build up a fiber optic system and then try to make revenue by having people hire space on it for things like long-distance calls, data file transfers, all the things that we use the internet for today. That was the asset approach: They would build their own segment from City A to City B, with more fibers than they needed, and then they'd trade the extra fibers for fibers somewhere else, like from City B to City C."

It wasn't long before Enron executives in Houston began to see it as more of a shorter-term money-making opportunity. "Houston noticed it looked sexy to the analysts because it had this communications aspect to it, and that's when Houston stepped in and said, 'We are going to run this like we are running the other businesses in Houston. . .We are going to try to get into bandwidth trading and we're going to try to distribute movies online, and we are going to amp this up and try to generate some return quicker.'"

It didn't take long after the leadership change before things began to fall apart. "What really ruined the communications enterprise was the fact that the Houston guys came in and tried to convert it to their own image. They didn't really know that much about communications and it didn't prove to be very wise choices they made in regard to some of these new efforts in the communications space."

Less than a year later Enron began dismantling the Broadband group. Luckily Erwin found an opportunity with the Portland office of his previous group, Enron Capital and Trade, and avoided having to move back to Houston. "That was my way out of Broadband as Broadband was being dismantled in Portland and re-concentrated in Houston, but it didn't last long in Houston either. . .That just fell apart, it was a disaster. Not enough people there knew what they were doing. The sad thing is that the broadband company had some great ideas, ideas before their time."

WATCHING ENRON FALL

At one point Erwin met a co-worker who told him something was wrong with the books. This co-worker had likewise been transferred to Portland from Houston and claimed it was because he had figured out that Enron was manipulating the numbers. "I didn't have the basis to judge whether or not there was a problem with the books, and I didn't know this guy well enough to know if I could completely trust him; so much was political, maybe he was a poor performer. How did I know? But he was the first contrary voice that I heard, and this was long before the bankruptcy."

The source warned, "It's all a house of cards, man, it's all going to fall down; you should sell your options." Erwin was skeptical but listened to the warning. "I think very few of us knew that Enron was near terminal, except that this guy suspected it, but he had a reputation as a squeaky wheel and I kind of discounted what he said, a certain amount."

To many who were heavily invested in Enron stock, it was hard to accept the news that this flourishing company was on its way to bankruptcy. They wanted to believe what they were hearing from their leaders; they were banking on it. "You know, it was like nobody wanted to believe it. . .the stock fell all the way to $40 or $50 and everyone still thought it would come back, and Skilling was telling us it would come back, and we didn't know any better."

As time went on and the negative media reports starting filling the airwaves, Erwin and his co-workers were astounded at how quickly things began to tank. "That fall was just a blur. It seemed unreal because it was so different from the flashy, successful, 'We figured out a new way and this is it,' and the arrogance that goes with it. That is so far away from the abject failure, 'We have nothing and we are going to file bankruptcy.' And yet we switched from one to other in probably just a couple of months."

When the dust finally settled, Erwin found his options and other investments that once totaled in excess of $500,000 were now completely worthless. "Some of it was lost company shares in the 401(k), but most of it was in stock options that I didn't exercise. . .We had special benefits in the Broadband group because of the go-go efforts that it had in the late '90s; the company gave the employees some unique benefits that the typical rank-and-file employee did not get, and one of them was restrictive stock: Every year another percentage would vest and you could own it then or sell it. I just didn't sell it. I was drinking the Kool-Aid."

Erwin sees the entire situation as being avoidable. "There's no reason Enron had to fail. Plenty of bright people, plenty of assets, plenty of good money-making businesses they were involved in, that if they just had a little more quality at the top in Houston, in my mind at least— maybe I am simplistic—they could have avoided these issues and the company could still be healthy today. That's the thing that made me so angry, because there were so many good bright people working there; it wasn't 60,000 criminals. And all those people had to go off and reinvent themselves, if they could."

ENRON AFTER BANKRUPTCY

For Erwin and his group, when the news came down that Enron had filed for bankruptcy, they had no idea if they still had jobs. "Your first question is, 'Do I still have a job?' I think they decided whom they needed to help during the first few months of the bankruptcy and they terminated some of us, and some of us just quit, and they offered the rest of us retention bonuses: If you stay X months you are going to get Y dollars. Until that happened, we all wondered if we would be summarily dismissed or what."

He watched as many people he worked with left voluntarily just before and after the bankruptcy. "A lot of people bailed; they didn't get laid off, but they left quickly around the time of the bankruptcy. I chose to stay because the economy was weak then. Portland doesn't have a lot of positions for lawyers in my area of expertise and I thought it might make more sense just to stay; I am really glad I did."

After everything settled down, working at Enron wasn't as difficult as it might have seemed. In fact, he enjoyed coming to work because of the new experiences he was exposed to. "The shock was pretty terrible. Once that wore off it was easy for me emotionally to come to work. I actually liked it. Since my deals weren't getting investigated, I didn't have to worry about them. I was interested to work with the government investigators, to help them figure out what happened; that was new and interesting to me."

As Enron was going through the bankruptcy process, some deals were discovered to be unethical or fraudulent; it was then that various government agencies became involved and those ongoing transactions had to be unwound, investigated and closed in some way. "The FBI and the Department of Justice and then these Attorneys General from several states were all involved and I got to work with them, which was really cool. I enjoyed doing that and again I was just helping them from the standpoint of figuring out what had happened and how to wind up these deals. That was a thrill."

ASSOCIATED WITH ENRON

Although it wasn't overt changes in behavior, he noticed to some degree a change in the way he was treated after Enron declared bankruptcy. "I remember going to meetings of all the lawyers in the company that would be held once every summer. When Enron Broadband was going great guns, people in the legal department I didn't even know would walk up and they would want to shake my hand and talk to me, almost like a rock-star thing, which was ridiculous, because I didn't deserve that and never had been that kind of a person, but yet a year later bankruptcy happened and you go and see those same people and they were much more reserved, even standoffish."

When the media started reporting on the scandalous behavior and hard-working employees losing their pensions, a stigma became attached to anyone who worked for Enron, before and after the bankruptcy. "It was weird; there was a little bit of guilt, I think. There's definitely disappointment with having been associated with an organization that had cheated its employees in such a way."

Both professionally and socially Erwin experienced a coolness towards him after others learned he was working for Enron. He learned to not take it personally and to brush off their off-handed comments and innuendos. "There's a fair number of people who lost money in Enron stock, nonemployees who had invested in the company and lost, and you could expect them to be bitter, just like I was when I lost money in WorldCom stock as an investor. Other people probably thought that all big business is dirty; there is some truth in that. Enron was just the latest example and they kind of curled their lip a little, and I get that."

As time went on and bigger companies failed, the stigma associated with Enron slowly faded into memory. "I think people kind of grew to realize there are two kinds of people at Enron: The kind who were good, and worked hard, and creative, and you wanted those, and then there were some rotten apples. I think over time it probably shook out okay. . .I don't think that it's anything that really hangs over today. One of the reasons why is that there have been so many huge failures since then, like WorldCom that was even bigger, and then you had everything associated with the financial disaster a couple of years ago—that all kind of pushes Enron off to the background."

LEAVING ENRON BEHIND

It took nearly two years to wrap up the book of business and close the chapter on Enron. For Erwin this time was filled with both anticipation and dread. "Grateful to have had the job during the two years of the bankruptcy period because that was the recession, and Portland's not a good job market for kind of the work that I do, so I was grateful to have had it."

He could tell the end was near and about six months before he left he began feeling out the job market. "I was hitting the online job boards and networking pretty heavily, knowing I would have to look for a job. But I didn't really know what to expect. I had always left the company I was working with; they had never kicked me out before."

It didn't take long before he learned that having Enron on his résumé wasn't exactly a good thing. "I can remember at the time that some legal recruiters saying it was definitely a negative, which was perplexing to me because I always thought that we were some of the best in terms of thinking up new ways to do things, with more creativity."

The comment made to Erwin by a corporate attorney he met who was employed by a major electronics manufacturer caught him by surprise. "He told me, 'You know, you really ought to just take Enron off your résumé.' Well, you can't do that, because that would be lying, and also I thought it was an incredibly weak comment by him; it showed how little he understood about Enron. You know you could have a half a dozen criminals at the top, but in our case there was an awful lot of good that was going on there too."

On December 1, 2003, he closed and locked the Portland doors of Enron for the last time. "Everybody was gone. I was kept busy until then; there was still a lot to do: winding up the deals, closing the book of business, helping with the investigations. . .All that work continued right up until the end, then the balance of it transferred to Houston."

ENDURING UNEMPLOYMENT

Erwin had always prided himself on having found new and better jobs before leaving the previous ones. He had felt fortunate to have secured the position at Enron just prior to the layoffs at his previous employer. This was the first time in his career that he was without a job. "It was kind of scary. I was not the right personality to enjoy time not working, as much as a better person might be. A person with a broader view than mine can probably just say, 'Well, something will turn up,' and just remain optimistic and really enjoy the time and find new things to do; I am probably a little more of a worrier than that. But, with a spouse who makes less, and two kids, I probably felt that I had to worry."

In preparation for the layoff and no job prospects, Erwin was faced with having to apply for government assistance to help them through this difficult time. "I applied for unemployment; that was the only time I had to do that, and we reined in our spending dramatically."

The assistance check amounted to only about $400 a week and the Erwin family ended up having to use their savings to make ends meet. "We have always been good savers; probably way outside of the norm, probably 25 percent savings rate every year since I got married. . . Nobody who saves wants to draw it down when they think of themselves as only in the middle of their career."

Thanks to the amazing survival stories passed down from his grandparents who had endured the Depression, Erwin had saved for hard times such as this. "All four of my grandparents made it through the Depression in the U.S. and they taught me the importance of avoiding non-mortgage debt and saving. . .For all we know, we may not have an income tomorrow."

Although Erwin learned from their example and was prepared financially for unemployment, he was not prepared for the emotional stress. "So we did save, but still, even if you do have savings and you are drawing it down and not knowing when you are going to find work, the mortgage is due every month and that's very heavy psychologically."

While Portland offers many amenities absent from a larger metropolitan area, it isn't the best place to be when you are an energy or telecom attorney looking for a job. "I am in a city where there just isn't a lot of industry. It's a great city for artists, not such a good city for business. And it took a long time, took about six or seven months, to get a part-time job with a company."

THE ENRON BOND

Erwin found that when it came down to it, those he knew from Enron really looked out for him during his time of need. "One of them gave me a job when he bought a small business and he hired me to help him do that. Several of them did a good job of just networking and staying in touch and suggesting job opportunities if they heard of them, that sort of thing, and made me feel connected and appreciated. I'm still grateful for it; I feel extreme loyalty towards every one of them and I'll never forget it."

It was a Houston co-worker who finally helped Erwin land that full-time job he was searching for. "He knew I was looking for work. . .and he suggested to a law firm in Portland that he was working with on behalf of Enron's post-bankruptcy business, that he knew this ex-Enron employee, me, who was looking for a job and if they knew of anything would they let him know."

Turns out that firm knew of a company that did have an opening and contacted Erwin. "They needed a temporary fill for one of the staff lawyers who was going out on maternity leave. . .I came in on what started as a temporary spot that within a month became a permanent spot, and now I've risen to General Counsel. So I have an Enron colleague to thank for that."

The bond runs deep on both sides of the fence as Erwin has in turn helped out former co-workers. "It goes the other way. I helped with references for several people, officer-level people and staff folks, who got jobs in other companies, and they landed really well on their feet. They would probably have done it just fine on their own, but I was happy to help them. I did what I could. . .It seems that most of the good jobs are not really advertised. You don't get jobs by responding to postings. You get jobs by letting people know that you want one, and if they think highly of you, if they know someone who likes you, the next thing you know someone is calling you—if you're lucky."

FINDING A BACKUP PLAN

The bitter taste of the layoff lingered even after he found a stable job. It never left his mind that one day he could again find himself unemployed. "I used to think, you got out of college, you got a job and you worked until retirement age and then you retired. Today it is much more complicated . . .companies don't tend to keep you around that long."

Erwin knows his years of experience are invaluable but also very telling. After looking at his résumé, it wouldn't take much to figure out his approximate age. "Once you pass a certain age, say 50 or 55, you start learning that age discrimination is very real. Maybe it's not that employers think we won't do a good job; maybe it is because that person costs too much to hire. But for whatever reason there is a de facto age discrimination going on, generally speaking. It's another reason to save while you're younger."

Taking all this into consideration, he knew he needed to take more control of his future. In 2007, Erwin decided to open a side business that satisfies his entrepreneurial spirit but at the same time provides an alternative if his corporate gig ever falls through. "I have a license from the state to buy wine from a winery or distributor and resell it to a consumer. I'm a commodities trader again. I have been doing that for a few years. I think part of my reason for wanting to was to create some independent source of income, even though it's very small compared to my day job, but it gives a feeling of a little bit more self-reliance."

He also takes steps in his everyday life to ensure he is ready for whatever challenge that may come his way. "That has taught me the importance of making hay while the sun shines, to state it one way; living beneath your means, and saving as much as you can when you do have a good job and you are making a good income. The Enron story certainly kind of pounds that lesson home more. If you're the kind of person who was making a good Enron salary, and you were living it up and stretching for more house than you could afford, then your personal wheels were really going to fall off when Enron failed. Versus the kind of person that would just squirrel away extra savings and enjoy it for what it was and just invest it; that kind of person wouldn't be hurt nearly so much."

WORDS OF ADVICE

Silver linings can outshine the black cloud. "So many good things have happened for me as a result of the Enron experience: I am in a city where I want to live, I've got great friends, I have great memories of very challenging work, and projects that expanded my abilities."

Personal growth hurts. "I learned the most when things were the worst. If you don't go through times like that, you don't know what you are capable of and maybe you aren't quite as wise as when you've gone through them. . .It is not like we want people to be exposed to terrible situations, but if you have to be, there must be something about the human condition that helps us to derive positive value out of it. I feel lucky, I'm happy, and I would have much rather gone through the whole Enron story than not."

FOR THOSE FACING A LAYOFF

Layoffs are business decisions. "Companies overreact to expected downturns and they lay off good people that they have to try to hire replacements for later, which is insane, but it's the new normal. It's a sickness in today's business. It's how businesses are handling themselves and for any victim of it, they just have to believe that it's not because of something they did wrong. There are obviously many exceptions to that, but by and large I think that's right."

"We all have big changes in our lives that are more or less a second chance."

-Harrison Ford

SIG ANDERSON

PORTLAND, OREGON – 2 YEARS

Enron Broadband Services (EBS) was the place to work; at least that is all Sig Anderson was hearing from his buddies who worked there. "They were talking it up: 'You gotta come over, it's some exciting stuff!' I went ahead and left the firm I was with and went to work for that group."

From that very first day Anderson knew he would have to keep up or be left behind. "There was just a lot going on: A lot of people didn't have much time for you, at least initially, until they figured out what you could do in the group. Just the way that things were run, it was really fast-paced, not a lot of structure to it. . .You walked in and checked in and, 'Here is your desk,' and you just went. I knew some people there, so that was helpful; I was in their group, so it wasn't like I was completely on my own."

EBS was expanding the physical network to Europe and he was intrigued. "The concept was to create a market in bandwidth to trade bandwidth, which was pretty progressive, pretty forward-thinking. In order to create a market they really needed a presence in the market. They needed fiber optic capacity in the U.S. and internationally if they were going to go global. They were going to install some POPs (Points of Presence) in the major European communication facilities."

Anderson immediately volunteered to help manage the project in London, England. "I signed up to the European role and I ended up being the U.S.-based project manager working with the European group. . . When we went over there, we stayed at a place called the 47 Park Street, a very exclusive hotel. I didn't know about it other people made the arrangements for me, and it was really expensive, it was around $440 a night, very high-end, very discreet."

The hotel was beyond any luxury the group had ever personally experienced. "We had a room that was like a suite. It had stuffed chairs and sofas; it had a full dining table where they could seat twelve people. . .It was palatial. It was like we should have giant parties there, but we didn't. We stayed there a couple of times and I remember getting back and thinking, here is a ten-day trip and a $13,000 bill. I thought nobody was going to pay for this expense report, but it sailed right through: 'Not a problem.' There were no guidelines; you could pretty much expense what you want."

Initially it was entertaining to rub elbows with the elite, but after a while Anderson's conscience began to bother him. "After two trips I thought it was so expensive, I just couldn't continue to do that. I went over and started staying at a nearby French hotel, and that was about half the cost and still a decent place."

After visiting the London offices, Anderson could hardly contain his excitement about being involved with EBS and the many possibilities that were continually opening up for him. "It was pretty impressive to see. You had screens over everyone's desk, big display panels up high and they would be watching all the world events and people would be trading energy there, live. It was all young people there and they were from all around the world, everyone has a flag of their home country at their desks—South Africa, Ireland, Argentina, Canada, you name it, everybody seemed to be represented there. . . They were trading energy contracts and futures and whatever, right there. It was a real big buzz going on there."

THE ENRON ATTITUDE

Enron acquired Portland General Electric (PGE) in the summer of 1997. Although on the surface the merger seemed complementary, within the company the two cultures never melded. Anderson felt fortunate to have worked under his boss, a former PGE employee. "He was extremely ethical and credible guy; he managed the construction of the long-haul fiber and stuff and the facilities. He was the rare square shooter there in the V.P. level."

Anderson could see a stark difference in leadership styles throughout the company. "That was good to be under him because there were some pretty squirrely operators in that whole company. It was the attitude they had picked up from the management, just the way it worked all the way down, Skilling and those guys. Portland was a little different; we weren't Houston-based. A lot of EBS employees were PGE to start with and our culture here was different. Houston was always trying to take everything to Houston and the Portland people were always trying to not take stuff down there, because they didn't want to relocate. There was always a natural conflict there."

He had witnessed firsthand their brazenness. "I remember going to a meeting there in Houston. It was the local little

Houston guys, short guys that were real cocky, and they were in there and they had somebody from London on the phone and they were just chewing this guy out: 'You can't do that without our approval! Who are you? Don't you know. . .?' I just sat there; I didn't know what was going on exactly so I couldn't really intervene. But I am sitting there and then they hung up the phone and they were so happy with themselves. 'We told them a thing or two!' and I thought, 'You two are going to get yours someday.' It was just awful, just an awful attitude; unbelievable."

CAUSE FOR CONCERN

It didn't take long before Anderson began to see problems with Enron's business practices. "After I studied the Mark-to-Market, they gave us some training, some financial training on it, I remember thinking, 'Wow, this is really aggressive! Is this really legal to do your accounting like this?' It was, but it never should have been."

About a year before the bankruptcy Anderson discovered he wasn't the only one with concerns. "People told me part way through, you know sometimes you get a feel that you could tell things aren't quite right, especially when the stock price started to come down. Somebody described it for me one time, 'This is like a treadmill, the minute it doesn't go faster, it stops. It always has to accelerate and if it doesn't accelerate then you're done.'"

During the summer of 2001, it became clear EBS did not have a sustainable business model and would be shut down. "About six months before they went bankrupt, they were already actively getting rid of EBS. I think they realized they couldn't really make a market in bandwidth like they hoped to. . .It looked good on the books for a while. They could put in fiber and trade fibers, but they would claim it as an income every time they did a deal. The fibers they kept they would claim as a long-term asset. So it looked like they were making money until they ran out of fibers."

Anderson watched as those around him were laid off and offered attractive severance packages. "I was hoping to get out in August 2001. . .They were going to keep ten people and lay everyone else off and I thought, 'GREAT, I am going to take my six-month severance.' But when we came into Portland that day they kept eleven people, and I was the eleventh because I was the project manager on a lot of stuff. They said, 'Oh, we are going to keep you around because you know what's going on.' I thought, 'Oh, just a few more months and I am out of here.' But it never worked out that way and they kept me until they went bankrupt. That was a kind of crappy period; I was really ready to go at that point."

WATCHING THE FINANCIAL CRASH HAPPEN

It all added up to a bad situation in Anderson's mind. He could see the end of Enron coming as clearly as day. "It became obvious. You could just watch the stock prices and if you studied their financials you could just see it was going to go all the way down."

There was little he could say to help those around him who continued to believe that the stock prices would eventually recover. "A lot of people didn't believe it would continue to decline. It was really interesting; I've seen a lot of stocks go all the way down. A lot of people would believe that every time the price would fall it was a better buying opportunity."

He remembers trying to warn people and many would shrug off his comments. He recalls people saying, "Well, it can't go below $30."

To which he responded, "No, it *can* go below $30."

And they would defiantly claim, "Oh, I don't think so; I am going to buy some."

There was little Anderson could say to convince them otherwise. "Some people continued to buy on the way down; they thought it had to go back up. But it was obviously not going to happen."

His voice quiets as he remembers the aftermath. "It was really sad to see people with options that were worth a lot of money that they never exercised at all. They always felt it would continue to go up. And of course when it didn't they continued to hold on, and at the end of the day they passed up on some pretty big, basically cash, payments. Unfortunately, a lot of these people had never had opportunities like this to get stock options like that; it was sad to see them fail. I know some people who were naive about investing."

Anderson's objective foresight might have been partly due to the fact that he wasn't personally at risk. "I never bought Enron stock and I didn't have a bunch of options, so I didn't have to worry about it. I didn't have that financial commitment that a lot of people did. Some people either received stock or bought a lot of it. Unfortunately, a lot of PGE had a lot of their retirement converted to stock. . .I came in from the outside, so I never had Enron stock. So in a way, it was just like a job to me."

THE WAITING IS OVER

Anderson started working for Enron with much enthusiasm. Towards the end, he could hardly muster the desire to go into work every day. He kept reminding himself of that handsome severance package waiting for him when that last day came. "You just wanted to get out. You were just waiting for whatever way 'to get out' was. We came in one day; we kind of knew there was going to be an announcement. They split us up and sent us all outside and said, 'We are retaining the other group to protect the assets, and the rest of you are laid off right now.' That was the end of it."

He had never felt so ready for the last day to come. With everything that had happened it was a relief to be finally done with EBS, but that sentiment was not shared by everyone in the group. "A lot of people were upset; it's just the normal trauma when you leave a job."

Having been laid off a few times before, Anderson was well prepared for the inevitable. "It had happened to me just a couple of times before. . .I had another job ready to go. I went back to a previous employer."

The generous severance package afforded to others never materialized. "I was hoping to get severance package at some point. . .That was where I got screwed. Give me six months of pay, wonderful! That was where I should have thrown a fit about being the number eleven and got out of there. But I was too accommodating."

AN IMPROVED SELF

Anderson's position at Enron exposed him to new areas and he had become more marketable. "I learned a lot about the telecommunications facilities and how that business works. Since then, the company I am back with now, my current consulting company, I work in the data center market, so a lot of stuff I learned at Enron in that broadband group has been helpful to me. It was really a good experience for me technically. It kind of broadened me."

His experience at Enron changed the way he looked at business. "It makes you a little more sensitive to business practices, ethical issues. You can see how quickly a business can grow. You can see the financial opportunities if you are at the right firm at the right time. I guess that is not that different from a lot of high technology firms."

WORDS OF ADVICE

Leave every job on a positive note. "Never burn bridges. Always be smart about what you are going to do. That is just being smart. I am surprised when people go out and light the place on fire. You never know how the next job is going to turn out. . .You need references; you need everything."

Look at the business objectively. "I definitely think you could see the signs if you watched what was going on and paid attention. You could see the ethical people and the not-so-ethical people if you looked hard enough."

Be a leader of your own destiny. "Keep your eyes open and use your critical thinking skills, and do not get sucked into the Kenneth Lay cult or whatever cult that is going on. Take a hard look at what is going on and make your own decisions. Keep from getting that groupthink, 'This is all going up, going up forever, blah, blah, blah!' I guess that comes with getting older. Be objective about what is going on and make up your own mind."

Know the difference between gambling and investing. "People who got hurt moneywise also got greedy. People who had options and sold them on a regular basis, methodically, and didn't try to hold everything to the end, always thinking it would go up, actually did pretty well. The people who thought, 'Oh, I will just wait another quarter, it will continue to go up and then I will do something'—of course, then it went down and a lot of them lost it all. Don't get too greedy; if you get a chance take your cash out when you can."

Keep a positive attitude. "You have to have fun as you do these jobs, whoever you are working for. We had our fun, got a lot done, did some pretty impressive things, but it all went down."

FOR THOSE FACING A LAYOFF

Get ready and be prepared before the layoff. "It's the basic stuff, you have to go back and start thinking about your options, clean up your résumé and get your contacts in line, and start making the phone calls so that you are pretty well prepared going out. I wouldn't wait until it's all done. You can start the wheels turning if you see it coming."

"The knowledge that a wise indulgent God is guiding events takes a weight of fear of blunders from the shoulders. Disappointments lose their sting because you feel that a greater wisdom than your own has decided the matter for you."

- Rev. Dr. Charles B. Swartz
Rhodes Scholar 1911 - Oxford University, Merton College

YUICHI SUDA

– PORTLAND, OREGON – 5 YEARS

*Y*uichi Suda was an accomplished international business consultant when he first came to work for Portland General Electric (PGE). "In 1995, I was working as a consultant to PGE. They were in the midst of dismantling the nuclear power plant, and they were sitting on a valuable piece of equipment which they were not ready to scrap."

While the equipment may have been valuable, it was costing them a lot of money to maintain. PGE consulted with Suda looking for a solution to the problem. Through his contacts and years of consulting experience, Suda was aware that many developing nations in the Pacific basin were facing a significant energy shortage. He asked, "Why not deploy that equipment instead of trying to find a buyer, and form a partnership with the utility in the Philippines, and build a power plant?"

PGE had not considered being an international utility company before and found the deal to be too tempting to pass up. Suda was offered a full-time position to structure and manage the deal. He had barely been working there a year when he detected a change within PGE. "I couldn't figure out what it was and it turns out there was a buyout approach from Enron from Texas, which was a transaction-oriented company."

Suda began to research Enron and found them to be almost exact opposites. "PGE was more thinking outside-the-box type of a company; Enron, very transaction-oriented rather than relational which is a utility. PGE valued more the relationship with clients, customers, and the local community—more so than growing the business or being profitable."

Their value systems did not match, but Enron knew PGE had something they didn't. "Based on what PGE was doing in the international market, they were stunned by how much we had established our presence in the market. They were going after the same project, as it turned out later; we did not know that."

Whenever Enron and PGE competed directly in international deals, Enron lost. "They have all these intellectual, smart, smartest guys coming out of business school, structuring, coming up with a business model, top notch, but when it comes to execution, they couldn't do it. Because they didn't have the relationship with whoever was offering the project, such as the local community, government, utilities and so forth."

PGE had what Enron lacked internally, "Enron was after PGE's so-called asset, quality-asset base—the long tradition of an engineer-driven company, hard-core American values and relationships. That was the missing link in the Enron culture."

ADJUSTING TO ENRON

Suda struggled to adapt to his new working environment. "I had to shift gears; it was like a panicky mode. In order for me to keep up with these young kids from headquarters, I have to shift gears and get things happening. They have this, 'Hey, I want that yesterday' type of approach. When you are in the relationship-building or the relationship-based business transaction, it takes time. Nothing like that happens overnight. But Enron's mentality, approach, was: I want that now, I wanted that executed yesterday."

It then became clear why Enron needed PGE, especially in certain cultures in the international market. "Enron was very much ME oriented, ME-focused business model, versus when it comes to dealing with Asia, in general, they will not talk to you unless they really get to know you, unless they get to have that trust underlying the relationship. Here Enron came across very arrogant."

CONQUERING JAPAN

In 1999, Enron had set its sights on deregulating the Japanese electricity market. "They put a lot of effort and political pressure on the Japanese utility regulators to open up. . .Enron was like a lobbyist behind the whole thing. They poured in quite a bit of money trying to convince everyone that deregulation was a good thing." They weren't making progress.

Suda remembers, "There were nine Japanese utility companies throughout Japan, and they thought, 'Who are you? As an outsider trying to change our game plan here, climate here, what are you trying to do?' Enron was looked upon as a rebel."

The Japanese did not trust Enron. The business community compared Enron's arrival in the Japanese market to the Black Ship commanded by Matthew Perry which arrived in Tokyo, Japan on July 8, 1853. This historical event forced Japan to open its ports to international trade for the first time in more than 200 years. "Enron was compared to this exact individual—Perry, the captain of the ship."

"There are some individuals who might have thought it was a good thing. When you try to break conformity in Japan, what you are doing is not healthy. So Enron was not looked upon as friendly, even though they couched it as such, saying, 'Hey, we are trying to form a partnership with you,' but it was a phony approach," Suda explains.

Enron lacked the resources to win Japan over. "Enron had no so-called tangible assets. In Japan, if you don't have tangible assets, or the reputation or the relationship, you can't do business; none of the individuals representing Enron during that time could show them anything tangible."

While youth or newness is a valuable commodity in the United States, it counts against you in the Japanese market. "Because Enron was a very new company, at that time had been in business only ten years, that was almost like a start-up company. The market value back then was $80 billion; that was significant. But how do you achieve that kind of evaluation being in business after only a little over ten years? So, people were just questioning, they were legitimate questions: 'What is your evaluation based on? You don't have any really significant tangible assets.'"

Suda was born in Japan and was intimately familiar with the Japanese culture. He was brought in to help with negotiations. "It was an uphill battle, just a struggle, to establish Enron's credibility. 'Hey, you may want to give it a second thought about this.'"

Suda melded Enron and PGE into one company and presented it to the Japanese market. "I played off PGE's longevity: 'Hey, we have been in business for over 100 years as a local utility. So I basically sold my credibility."

This worked because all nine utilities in Japan had a solid working relationship with PGE. The doors began to open and the opportunity was there for Enron to approach the bargaining table. "That was a part of my job responsibility, to cultivate that relationship."

PUTTING IT ALL ON THE LINE FOR ENRON

Even after Suda became the face of Enron, the Japanese continued to be suspicious. Suda was trusted, but not Enron. "Having been born and raised in Japan, I knew what it took to do business. Being with them, they were looking at me really strangely and implied, 'What are *you* doing here?' They would pull me aside and say, 'Who are you? Why are you working with them?'"

Suda went right to work trying to solidify a lucrative deal to bring video-on-demand to Japan between Nippon Telegraph and Telephone Corporation (NTT), Sony, Blockbuster, and Enron. The agreement was that NTT would provide the high-bandwidth internet connection, Sony would provide the technology and the production of the set-top box to receive and transmit the information, and Blockbuster would provide the content. "It never booked because bankruptcy killed it, but we got to the point of, 'Yes, let's move forward.'" This was in August of 2001.

Suda's voice is filled with amazement, sadness, and some anger as he recalls what he thought would be the crowning moment of his career. "But it was all hot air; there was no substance underneath. Here I was in the Japanese market with all these top business leaders and we were negotiating a major business collaboration. It was exciting; I was proud; it was quite an accomplishment to bring all these significant people to the table."

Although words were never said, Suda remembers not all parties were as optimistic as he, "But you could also tell, though, this sense of skepticism in the face of the Sony chairman: 'What's beyond this? I am having a hard time putting my finger on it but something is not right.'"

Suda returned from his trip in Japan to find that everyone in his department had been laid off except himself. "The layoffs started happening here in Portland in July. It started trickling, with the direct business unit, support group. They were let go and started downsizing, and then the major shift started happening in September. When I came back from Japan, I remember sitting in my office at River Place and seeing those vacant desks. I remember it was September 11 and the television was on. It was an eerie feeling, in a ghost building and watching the events unfolding—the twin towers in New York."

He stood alone as he watched his co-workers pack up and leave. "There were a handful, about twelve to fifteen people; everybody was packing. But for some reason I was never let go because I was still working on that transaction. So that was a double-edged sword, in a way. Because I was not let go, I was not able to get the package the people were granted back in July, August, and September."

His emotions were in conflict as he took in all the unfolding events. "I felt insecure in a way that, 'Hey, what is going on?' But also I wanted to finish. I don't like to walk away with a project half-baked. I put my whole heart and soul into this from the beginning, so I wanted to complete it; that was my feeling. I kept working, and management from Houston encouraged me to stay on and try to book that transaction as quickly as possible."

LOSING MORE THAN A JOB

Suda worked diligently and managed to close one last deal before being laid off from Enron. "I was also working on another transaction—selling bandwidth to Japanese TV to broadcast the Winter Olympics. They were going to do the first live broadcasting through the fiber optic cables."

He had also accumulated between $18,000 and $20,000 in travel expenditures on his corporate American Express card in the previous three months. "I had still not yet finalized my exit package, severance package and so forth. I began to start dealing with Houston. I was told that if I hurry up and submit the expense report, then I would be okay. But I did not have everything in my Excel because I still had some pending business-related expenses in Japan, and so I waited until mid-December to submit it."

In addition to losing his job, Suda realized the future he had worked so hard to secure for his family was gone. "Yes, I not only lost a job, but I also lost our sons' college savings for tuition. Because I stayed longer than the rest of the employees who left with a severance package, I was shut out. I could not exercise any of my stock options that I had set aside for their education."

Attempting to salvage some money due him, Suda contacted Enron to check on his reimbursement status. "Because it was already in bankruptcy, they said, 'No, we are not in control anymore. It is in the hands of the bankruptcy court.' So, if you were an employee back then, you were on the bottom of the stack. The attorneys and CPAs got paid first, then creditors. Employees and employee-related liabilities were at the bottom."

"In the meantime I started getting phone calls from American Express. They said as long as my name was on it, it didn't matter; as a corporate American Express client, I was liable." Suda immediately contacted an attorney to investigate the validity of their claim.

"I contacted an attorney and they said that's true what they were saying. I need to negotiate with them in terms of a payment schedule; I had to structure a two-year payment schedule." He knew he needed to quickly find employment to keep afloat.

Suda looked to PGE, but "by then all the positions and job openings at PGE, because people had gone back to PGE to seek employment, everything was filled. July, August, all those groups prior to my departure, they went back and so I couldn't find a job."

He tried every means possible to find another job but he couldn't even secure an interview. He learned that it might have been because Enron was on his résumé. "One consultant that I ended up talking to recommended I downplay Enron and mention only PGE. He was not encouraging me to lie about it on my résumé, but, 'Yeah, you were working for PGE, so therefore hyphen-ate it "PGE-Enron" and see how that's going to play.'" It didn't work.

In February he started his own company to resurrect his international consulting career, only to find he had been blacklisted. "I could not find anything in Japan. My reputation and credibility went to zero, nothing."

A NEW BEGINNING

Suda lost more than just money when Enron collapsed, but he sees it as a positive turning point in his life. "In a way, it was blessing in disguise. What happened after the bankruptcy, it improved my relationship with my wife and the family. You can't go on regretting what's lost, but you can turn that into something positive, what you can do for a better future."

He sees no value in living a money-centric life. "Yes I did make a lot of money during that short period, but when you make money and you are on that fast track, you spend it. I can't think of anyone who saved more than they spent. You know, that is the kind of sinful nature that lives among us all. Isn't it? You make more; you end up spending more, especially when you are on the fast track. It is very difficult to look beyond that and think about the future because you are living in that moment."

He thanks God for saving him from a doomed future. "I believe every experience has a purpose in my life, and I saw this as a turning point for my faith. I think it was God that was trying to tell me, 'Hey, I think you are going down a wrong path here.'"

A STRONGER FAMILY

When Enron filed for bankruptcy, not only was Suda affected, but his wife and two sons felt the impact as well. In a moment, everything Yuichi and his wife Gail had worked for was taken, and the only things left to cling to were God and each other. Together they stood firm as their lives crumbled around them. In the end, they were stronger and happier than they ever expected to be or ever would have been had they never endured this hardship. To this they can only say, "Thank you, Enron."

Christmas was only a few weeks away when the Suda family realized their dire financial situation. Their children sensed the tension and through their innocent words reminded them how truly blessed they really were. Gail remembers, "Our younger son, Kevin, age 13, said, 'Mom, what would you like for Christmas?' Realizing we weren't going to have any money to spend on presents this year, I said, 'The best thing you can give me is something you write.' To this day, his poem entitled 'A Mother's Love,' and his brother Ryan's 'Dear Mom' poems are the two most precious gifts I have ever received from anyone."

They were offered a rare and true glimpse into the hearts of those around them. Gail explains, "When something as traumatic as Enron happens, family and friends either come on strong or they turn away. Naturally, we expected our families to show they cared, but we never expected friends to show such generosity. As the months and years progressed, it was made clear to us who really loved us in ways we had never experienced. Friends and family reversed roles. It is truly humbling to be told, and shown by unbelievable acts of kindness and generosity, 'We love you . . .we are here for you.'"

Yuichi and Gail were forced to make some hard decisions. One of them was to leave the only home their children had ever known. Gail remembers, "We had to sell the house we had owned for 22 years and move to a rental townhouse. Cleaning out what we had accumulated over these years was both emotional and freeing. We had to downsize from 3200 square feet to 1500 square feet. We had to move across town and leave the familiarity of our neighborhood. To our utter surprise, we are truly much, much, happier in our new place than we were in our old neighborhood. . .I don't dwell on what was, but look forward with eager anticipation to what lies ahead."

Kevin and Ryan could not be sheltered from the harsh realities. When their college savings account evaporated, they were forced to clear their own paths in life. It turned out to be the best gift a father could ever give: the gift of independence. Gail explained, "Our two sons have learned a lot from how their father and I coped with life's unpleasantness. They had to grow up quickly and realize they alone were responsible for their futures. Both boys worked hard in college to make lives for themselves apart from us. Mom and Dad could not financially support them after graduation, so they had to get and keep a job. They are both financially independent and exceedingly happy in their personal lives."

Sometimes in order for new life to grow, the old life must be cleared away. Gail used this opportunity to explore all her options and ended up discovering herself. Gail said, "I have returned to the world of work. I have a master's degree in social work, but after taking 22 years off to raise our boys, I have had to shift gears. Now, I am a nationally-certified pharmacy technician and love being back in the workplace. I enjoy having a place where I am needed and work that is interesting."

WORDS OF ADVICE

Be careful if you are too busy to think. "When you feel that you are put on the fast track escalator and you start feeling like you have a loss of control—that is a warning sign. The best way to control people and their minds is to keep them busy. They don't question. They have no time whatsoever to question or think about anything but trying to execute that transaction. I was on that escalator. I knew I didn't want to stay on that escalator; it was going too fast, and I could not get off of it. Being busy is very sexy in a way, because you are flying everywhere all around the world at the company's expense. You are living the lifestyle, busy. It's a very flashy lifestyle, and when you are making good money, you lose sight of what is really important in your life. So, if anyone out there is still continuing to live in the ME world, I think it's time to reflect, step back, and reevaluate."

Build your trust in God. "I was fortunate that I was brought back to my senses as I was going down the wrong path. If I did not have the opportunity to build on my faith, I don't know, I might have committed suicide. Who knows? Even though I think it was a healthy transition, it was a painful transition. But when you end up pursuing and building your treasure instead of His, you have to face the consequences."

Servants make the best leaders. "If you really want to be a leader, you really need to serve people before you lead. You can't skip the process of serving and teaching. You can't expect anyone to just follow you without serving them first. That's the major mistake Enron made. They tried to create that phony relationship with the phony compensation package. They basically fed the money into their system thinking it was going to create leadership. That is not the way you create leadership. Certainly that servitude leadership model was not coming down from the top."

FOR THOSE FACING A LAYOFF

Look for the hidden reason. "I would look at it as a positive. I would look at it as an opportunity to transition to something that is more meaningful. I think if you are a faith-driven individual, God is telling you something."

Take time before rushing on to the next job. "Reflection and reevaluation are really important if you are faced with a layoff or any kind of transition. Try to see if what you are experiencing right now is giving you an opportunity to take your life in another direction."

"Certainly it is most important how a person takes his fate than what it is."

-Wilhelm Von Humboldt

MICHAEL LECHNER

SAN RAMON, CALIFORNIA – 1 YEAR 3 DAYS

*M*ichael Lechner was working full-time as a consultant but only had one client. "It was a really good client, but the client's funding was from year to year, so my problem was, if funding didn't come through I was on the street looking for another job. I let my client know that this wasn't really the kind of secure future that I was interested in."

He began asking around and a colleague suggested he look at Enron. "They are hiring good people all the time." She explained, "You're a shoo-in; you'll be perfect for a position in San Ramon."

After some research, Lechner realized he had found exactly what he was looking for. "I thought, 'Holy cow, this was a dream come true! This is just the type of company I'm looking for. . .so a few phone calls later I was in their offices in San Ramon and going through the interview process."

Enron wasted little time. "A week and a half later I had a job offer. I went to my client and said, 'I really hate to dissolve our relationship, because you have been good to me and I enjoy the work and everything, but this opportunity has come along with Enron and it's obviously the kind of opportunity I have been looking for that can't be delivered in the current situation. So, I went off to Enron."

HELLO ENRON

During the interview process, Lechner had been given a tour of the building. It was like nothing he had ever seen before. Enron leased two floors of a large building in San Ramon. One floor was dedicated to the engineering company that Enron had recently purchased. The upper floor was only half occupied, as Enron anticipated the other half to be filled when Enron Broadband moved in. "I thought, 'Wow, I had fallen into just the right place here. This is so cool: latest computers, latest everything, brand spanking-new stuff all around.' Of course, tons and tons of very excited people."

It was all happening so fast and his head was still spinning when he and his wife were encouraged to attend the annual Christmas party. "I was hired a few days before Thanksgiving in 2000. My boss at the time said, 'Oh, you'll want to make airplane arrangements for you and your wife to attend the annual Christmas party in Houston. They throw this big shindig every year.' Literally, we had been with the company for three days and she and I got on an airplane and flew to Houston."

It seemed Enron was exceeding any expectation Lechner had of a company. He couldn't believe his good fortune. "Talk about wow factor! They had a mammoth Christmas party, the likes of which I have never seen—again refortifying this idea that I'd made the right move to this huge company that knew what it was doing. We were enormously impressed by this Christmas party."

SEEING PROBLEMS

Lechner soon began to question Enron's viability. "After about six months, there was a small group of us account managers in the commodity electric sales arena who were starting to say, 'You know, this is looking a little peculiar to us.' Of course the regulatory environment was starting to come undone at that time in California, and we started asking ourselves questions like, 'How are we making money doing what we're doing?'"

Enron had anticipated being able to make money by purchasing electricity at a bulk rate. "It had acquired Pacific Gas and Electric's (PG&E) Energy Services book of accounts that were fixed-price contracts. But as we were serving them, it became apparent that there was no way we could meet that price. It was a discounted five percent off whatever the utility bill was. . .We started to realize that something didn't feel quite right."

The price of electricity continued to rise but Enron was bound by the fixed-price contracts and had to eat the difference. As time went on, Enron began running out of money. "As the regulatory world started getting worse, of course jacking up the prices and things like that, what we saw happening was more and more irritated Enron customers.. . .We started to see PG&E turning off their services because Enron wasn't paying the bill."

This put Lechner in the worst position possible: the middle. "I dreaded as an account manager every time my cell phone or my pager went off because I knew it was an irate customer calling to complain. I was supposed to fix their problems but was not getting the kind of support from Houston that we needed to solve the situation."

One large brand-name hamburger chain had signed up every one of their stores, including franchise-owned, to be serviced by Enron. This umbrella contract had over 400 different customers. Lechner was the account manager assigned to that contract when PG&E began disconnecting services. "I had received phone calls from some rather irate customers that had indeed had their electricity turned off, and they said, 'We're going to have to sue you. You are putting us out of business! We can't run our operation if we aren't assured power. Now we have to go to PG&E and plead with them.'"

He had always taken great pride in offering personal customer service and doing everything possible to make sure problems were solved. This time he was powerless to act; all he could do was listen and watch. "People were haranguing me. Now, I have been around the block a time or two, and knew not to take it personally, but it was abundantly clear that the company I thought was the rocket ship to the moon was failing its most important asset—its customers. . .Talk about falling a notch or two down from 'I am walking on water' to 'Holy cow, what's going on here? I'm drowning!'"

SEEING THE END

In the months leading up to the bankruptcy, Lechner began to hate his job. "When my phone would ring or my pager would go off, my heart would sink; it was hell, in a word. It is not the kind of environment that is conducive to jumping out of bed in the morning and saying, 'I can hardly wait to get to work; I'll skip breakfast.' Terrible."

About two or three months before the office closed, Lechner and his co-workers knew it was just a matter of time.

"We heard rumors that the broadband division wasn't living up to expectations and was being shut down. . .They started letting people go, right and left, and of course, that coupled with the debacle of the energy sales. . .It was abundantly clear that Enron was headed south fast. We were instructed not to let the customers know what was going on."

A few weeks before the closing, Lechner said to his boss, "I can see the handwriting on the wall. May I suggest that we instruct everybody to take anything out of the office that is personal? That way we don't have to fight to get back in if we get here one morning and the doors are locked.' 'Good idea,' he said. So we instructed everybody in the office to take plants, to take books, to take memorabilia, anything out of the office that you didn't want to lose but wasn't company property."

Everyone in his department was owed substantial sums of money for expense reports they had submitted, expecting reimbursement. Lechner and his peers grew more concerned. During a meeting Lechner offered an alternative form of payment. "I said, 'You know what? You owe me several thousand dollars. I am somewhat inclined to not return my computer to you as a kind of account payment for that.' They said, 'No, really you can't do that. . .We are working at getting you your reimbursement checks when they close the doors. You need to leave everything that is company property behind.'"

FINALLY LAID OFF

At 8:30 a.m., an all-hands meeting was announced and the remaining seven employees reported to the big conference room. As Lechner waited to hear the formal announcement, he thought back to the first meeting he had attended just over a year ago. "I remember being in that room with all the other employees and upper management together. I looked around and thought, 'Holy cow, there are a lot of people in this room, at the table and in and around the periphery of the room as well.'"

He was amazed by how very different matters were just one year later. "Here we are in this mammoth room, big conference-room table, lots and lots and lots of empty chairs, with now seven people and this person from Houston saying, 'Sometimes these things happen. . .at 10:00 we expect you to have vacated the building and the doors will be locked.'"

There were no reimbursement checks to be handed out, striking fear in the hearts of all who remained. "Everybody was very concerned about that. Some people were far more in the hole than I and were very concerned, $5,000, $7,000 in business-travel expenses. . .but to be told, 'We are working on it, stay tuned, we'll get it to you,' is not a lot of comfort from this huge company that just slammed the doors on their employees."

Remembering the severance packages offered to those who had been terminated earlier in the year, one person asked when they could expect to receive their package. To that the Houston representative responded, "We're bankrupt; we are filing for bankruptcy. So, the chance you are going to get a severance package is virtually nil."

At 10:00 they all left the building and headed to a nearby Mexican restaurant. "We all sat around the table and said, 'Well, at least six months ago, when we talked about this not being a sustainable business model and kind of watched it disintegrate, wasn't it smart of us to be right?

Isn't it a shame we were right?' Now, six months later we were on the street looking for jobs. We were all in the same boat. Everybody pretty much had the same talents and capabilities."

A few hours later they wished each other luck as they left the restaurant to face an uncertain future. "We were all off to look for new jobs in an economy and market that wasn't really very good for what we had to offer. . .Some of the people had either connections or had lined up work even earlier than that. I think one or two of them had jobs at the time Enron closed its doors. I did not; four or five of the other people didn't. So we went off in our own directions and started looking for work.

FINANCIAL IMPACT

About six weeks after the being laid off, Lechner's reimbursement check arrived. "Which was comforting, but I had written off any kind of severance package. Over the course of the years with the lawsuits, I've seen checks dribble in as settlements have been reached and arrangements made. . .The settlements over the years never made up in total for what it would have been according to company policy, but at that point it didn't matter. Anything was appreciated, small as it might have been. I wasn't expecting anything anyway."

Compared to others, he felt fortunate. "I came away, as things went, basically unscathed. I had my 401(k) that had come with me. . .I didn't have money invested in Enron stock. I'm not sure if it was a conscious decision on my part, or whether I'd been in this position before where the talk didn't quite fit the circumstances: the hyping of the company stock. Certainly it was on a stellar rise when

I first went to work there; it was like $80 a share. I didn't really pay attention to it, but in six months it had gone up, like, thirty percent."

It was understandable why so many had bought Enron stock. "I was in an all-hands meeting in Houston where Ken Lay was saying, 'Oh, you buy stock, it is going to go through the roof', and all of that kind of stuff. Afterwards he was telling people to buy, and the Employee Stock Ownership Program was frozen so employees couldn't sell stock. It was another kind of ice pick in the side, so to speak, to people getting burned because they put so much faith in the company."

It still amazed Lechner how quickly he had gone from feeling on top of the world, working for an amazing company with lots of potential, to standing in the unemployment line. "You can think you've got everything sewn up, and the rug can be pulled out from underneath you at a moment's notice."

He had been laid off before and knew not to take it personally. "I have not lost faith in myself. It's a shame the company bought the farm, but it's no reflection on me. Other people may have taken it harder, certainly, but because of my previous experience, it was sad, but it wasn't a life-changing experience."

LOOKING FOR NEW EMPLOYMENT

Lechner found himself looking for a job at the worst possible time. "Options were limited in the job market in general in California, and the electricity job market in particular. With the skyrocketing electricity prices, Enron's filing for bankruptcy, PG&E filing for bankruptcy,

Southern California Edison narrowly escaping that fate, and the 'dot-com' bubble bursting, a lot of companies were just trying to hang on."

The California legislature, their deregulation of the electric market in failure mode, put a moratorium on signing up any new direct-access electric customers. "Jobs in the energy sector, precisely the kind of experience I had in spades, dried up fast." Lechner would either have to find something existing or get into a new field.

He contacted the client he worked for just prior to Enron. "When I left that client to work for Enron, it was done on very agreeable terms. I went back to that client, and they were aware of what was going on as well. I said, 'Apparently, I've got some time on my hands, so if you are interested in me doing some additional work for you, I'm available.'"

Lechner was immediately accepted, but in a different capacity than before. "A new contract was put in place for me, not at the level it was before, but it allowed for some part-time work, some fill-in work, some interesting stuff I had never been involved in before. I treaded water for a while on that contract and looked for other clients over the course of time, looking for a more permanent position that had the kind of security that I thought I was going to have working for Enron."

He tried everything possible to stand out of the crowd. "I actually hired a company to help me write my résumé. I figured I would look to professional companies that do résumés and do training—relearn how to get into the job market now that it had been changed by the Internet. I had applied for a large number, maybe 50 to 75 jobs, on the Internet. I can't recall ever getting a single response."

Lechner eventually quit wasting his time on job boards and went back to what he knew would work best. "Over time, what I started to realize was that the Internet was not going to work for me, that I would have to go out and find some type of connections and networking as a means of finding a position. . .In the end, I was out of a job for about a year doing this pick-up, part-time work for this client. When I finally got a job, it was through networking."

A NEW PERSPECTIVE

After leaving Enron, Lechner continued to receive phone calls from former customers. "It wasn't exactly legal advice; I think they were more looking for a shoulder to cry on. . .It was a ghastly situation, and these people, I guess, in some respect appreciated the fact that I was concerned about them enough that they would call back later and say, 'This is what happened to me; do you remember the chain of events? Would you mind talking to our lawyers about this?' So, in retrospect I guess did a fairly good job, at least with those customers, in seeing their plight and trying to help them out. It was clearly a mess that would have required a lot of help."

Lechner watched, mildly fascinated, as the leaders of this great company went on trial. Ultimately, what saddened him most was to learn that Enron crumbled for such stupid reasons. "I had met all those folks on my trips to Houston. . .I still to this day do not know if Ken Lay knew what was going on and if he was a tremendous actor, or was clueless and caught up in this event that he thought couldn't possibly happen. All in all, I feel sorry for those people, but at the end of the day you make your bed."

Lechner sees a bright spot in all of this. "There were seven people in our office when they closed the door at Enron. To this day, all the ones that I interact with from that time period are dear friends. It was kind of a bonding experience, if you will. . .In the grand scheme of things, I don't think you could come away with a better outcome than that, because that's really what's important."

WORDS OF ADVICE

Change is the only constant. "Realize that the world isn't always necessarily fair, and to the extent you can, try to prepare yourself for these kinds of events. That's something that you should keep in mind. Just because you think you have it really, really, good, doesn't mean it's always going to be that way."

FOR THOSE FACING A LAYOFF

Reductions don't discriminate. "If you get laid off in a situation such as this, when clearly a very large number of very dedicated, very good people were terminated from a company they believed wholeheartedly in, you cannot look at it as a reflection on your character or your own personal well-being. Obviously you are out of a job, but it shouldn't be internalized as something you did or a reflection on your personality or capabilities."

"Your worth consists in what you are and not in what you have; what you are will show in what you do."

-Thomas Davidson

ROB DAVIS

COSTA MESA, CALIFORNIA – 2 YEARS

ob Davis was a Major Account Manager for Enron Energy Services (EES). He came to Enron with many years of experience in the utility industry. "I am a third-generation utility industry guy. There was a point in time when my father, my grandfather and I all worked for Southern California Edison. At one point we were all at the same property, at the same time . . .The last company I was with pre-Enron, I was in power quality doing consulting. We were an engineering consulting firm."

One day he was offered the opportunity by a friend to come to a 'lunch and learn' at the Enron offices. "While I was there, I participated in the meeting, I asked questions. At the end of the meeting, one of the managers asked me if I was interested in a job. He explained to me that EES had just started to get its head of steam then, they were going to be hiring for some folks to be that intermediary between the engineering group and the construction group."

THE PERFECT ENERGY SOLUTION

Davis had never before seen a utility company bring in both sides, the supply and demand, to the customer. It had always just been about supply, making sure the customer had power and billing them for that service. Now, Enron was bringing them power but also providing a way to lower their monthly bills and conserve energy by upgrading and installing fixtures that increased efficiency and reduced consumption. There was great demand by the consumer for reducing the cost of energy. "It made perfect sense. We were not only advising them, the customer, what to do, but also doing it for them. It was really something to see."

True to Enron fashion, they did not dawdle about hiring him. "By the time I got back to my office, which was about a 45-minute drive from there, I had an offer in my email. Opened it up, took a look at it, and my reaction was, 'Holy smoke, you want to pay me that much to do this? Yeah, I will be right down!' Within a couple of weeks, I was over there. Enron had something special going on. The whole process of discovering it and becoming a part of it, in very fast order, was impressive."

For two weeks, Davis was trained on the energy-efficiency concept and introduced to the inner workings of Enron. "There were a lot of resources committed to the whole process of getting people on board. Getting people to understand what the value proposition of the company was. I was really impressed. From what we could all see, our efforts would be extremely well capitalized. There was money everywhere. It was all investor dollars, turned out. But at the time, I was very confident that I had gone someplace very special."

The caliber of individuals was nothing like Davis had ever experienced before. "For me it was very cool. There were some bright, bright people there. It was not unusual to be in a room with a bunch of military academy graduates or retired generals. They were the best of the best. They were the cream of the crop. But that was why they were there. These people achieved in everything they did."

Down to the last detail, it appeared Enron had thought of everything. "I remember my first day. I was impressed when I got there—Enron, they liked that whole cubicle thing—my cubicle was stocked. Everything was there, I didn't have to go figure out where things were; it was well thought out. Everything was there, ready to go. 'Okay, go do it!'"

A SWEET DEAL

"One of the things that made EES's offering compelling was the fact that they were using Enron capital, Enron's cash, to finance these projects." This practice was previously unheard of. Usually companies lacked the capital necessary to finance such an endeavor and required the customers to fund the upgrades. Years later the customers were able to realize the return on their investment. That is what made Enron's offer so appealing to the customer. They couldn't lose. Enron would finance the upgrades and guaranteed a reduction on the customers' electric bills. It wasn't exactly a hard sell.

Enron would become the customer of record with their clients' utility accounts. Enron would receive the bill, pay it and pass on the bill, minus the guaranteed discount, to the customer. The question then begs to be asked: How did Enron expect to make money? Their thinking was, if they signed up enough clients, they would be able to purchase electricity at the bulk rate, thus reducing their costs by a small percentage. Additionally, with the new energy efficiency upgrades, Enron would see a lower electric bill.

"Enron would look for projects that would drive additional savings below that guarantee savings," Davis explains.

The problem was it took about two years to get the project up and running. During this time, Enron was paying utilities the full amount and being reimbursed only at the discounted price, plus paying the costs associated with upgrading the facility. Even with everything working according to plan, it would take roughly seven years before Enron started to realize a profit. "They were doing this by the droves; tens of millions of dollars were being poured into these facilities."

One might ask why this was a problem. The idea was great, but these types of investments require lots of capital. In order to continually bring in new funding, they needed to show investors that they were turning a profit every year. Through the use of Mark-to-Market accounting, Enron could realize the projected profits that first year. "What they would do, they would sign a 10-year deal, take the projected earnings for that contract, and bring all those earnings forward. They would take the adjusted 10-year value for that earnings report on year one."

This in theory is great, but assumptions were being made when calculating those earnings. It assumed that the baseline use for the customer would remain constant, the price per kilowatt would remain stable, and the costs of installation and upkeep of the energy-efficient upgrades would never change. More importantly, the sales staff had to sign up more customers than the year before to continually show an increase in annual profits. "Basically, you had to double sales every year to seem like you are making money."

Enron had so many people signing up that it was a daily struggle to keep on top of the work load. "In the project side or delivery side of the house, we existed in a frantic pace to walk all these customer sites, develop all these projects, obtain all the approvals from the customer, and then the internal folks had to approve. It was miserable. I mean, I enjoyed it, but from the standpoint of the business, but we all knew that this was not sustainable."

Davis didn't fully understand the business or even how they were making money; he believed those above him saw the whole picture and were steering the company in the right direction. "It was new to everybody; it was new to me. I had been a contractor, been in construction, even working for a utility. These unique revenue reporting or accounting practices just didn't make sense to me at all."

EXPERIENCING THE INEVITABLE

EES terminated a majority of its workforce in the summer of 2001. On December 1, Davis was asked to stay with Enron and spin off into a new subsidiary. On December 3, EES officially declared bankruptcy, but the new subsidiary was not involved. Everyone in the group was confident their new venture was destined for success. "So there was no thought in my mind that I was going to get whacked. I wasn't amazed that it could happen, but it just didn't seem like it was going to happen at that point. So it was as if I had dodged a bullet. In the short period of time that we were up and running, we were making things happen, getting projects back on line; we were doing well."

About the second week in December, his boss called an impromptu meeting right around lunchtime. "I didn't think much of it because he had done that type of stuff like in the past; it usually meant he had brought in sandwiches or pizza. It also meant that we were having a project meeting and he often used those kinds of occasions to say, 'Okay, what's going on in your world?' I wasn't alarmed."

Davis took a seat around the conference table along with everyone else in the office. Sitting alongside Davis's boss was the president of EES, from Houston. In a flat tone his boss said, "Okay, Jeff, they're all here."

Everyone quickly realized something significant was going on. All eyes turned to the president as he began to explain, "Hate to be the one to tell you this but we got pulled back into the bankruptcy. . .and you're all gone."

The bankruptcy judge had ruled this new subsidiary was a party to the Enron bankruptcy. Everyone was terminated. Davis was given one hour to gather up his things and leave. He was in complete shock. About thirty minutes before-hand, he had closed escrow on a new house. "I was 36, two little kids, brand-new house. My wife was only working part-time. She was a schoolteacher and she was sharing a contract. We had stretched ourselves, like people do when they move, into the house that we knew we would be in for a while. It had a pool. We took that leap of faith, that big stretch."

As Davis was packing up his car, he was flooded with emotions as the reality of the situation began to sink in. He dreaded his next task—breaking the news to his wife. "That was bad. It was like, okay, I mean, I knew I would survive, it wasn't cancer, but what do I say when I get home? I had changed employers in the past, that wasn't a big deal, but I had never come home saying, 'Guess what?'"

THE FINANCIAL IMPACT

Enron offered many incentives to new employees investing in Enron stock. "When I came onboard I was offered this opportunity: If I rolled my 401(k), built up over twenty years in the workforce previously, all into Enron stock, they doubled it. I rolled $100,000. I ended up with $300,000 right away. They gave you similar kinds of opportunities during bonus time. If you did that same thing and chose to go with all Enron stock in the offering, they would double it or one-and-a-half it; they'd throw a lot at it. I think went through two of those, plus I contributed regularly while I was there."

When the stock started to fall, Davis could only sit back while everything he worked for over twenty years disappeared. "We had been watching our 401(k); they switched administrators during a time that the stock was crashing, so people couldn't do anything with their 401(k)."

He laughs now, but at the time it made him sick to his stomach. "I think I was already well into having lost every bit of what I had rolled into it anyway. The day of the layoff [December 3], there really wasn't much there. By comparison, the 401(k) shock had already happened. For all of us that were still invested in it, it was gone. We used to sit at lunch in a deli nearby that always had CNBC on, and watch the bloodbath."

While on paper the loss was devastating, Davis wasn't as concerned about it at the time. "I didn't think of it as something that I wouldn't recover from. Because we were still getting paid, we had dodged a bullet to stay employed, so that money wasn't real money at 36 years old. It wasn't contributing to my lifestyle."

When Davis was still working for Enron, he thought the stock would eventually recover and he could recoup the paper losses. "I knew that the 401(k) money was gone. We knew it was gone. We still had our shares, so there was still hope. We were doing something, it was still Enron; get through this thing and maybe there will be something. I felt pretty confident that we had a business model that made sense. If we could get out from under this mess, get this part behind us, we could start hitting stride again and be okay."

When he was laid off, he knew the loss was permanent. "When we were told, 'Out of here,' it was obvious that nothing good was going to come of it."

FINDING THE NEXT OPPORTUNITY

The one thing that saved Davis was the real-estate transaction. "We had sold the house and bought the house we are currently in. We had timed the real estate market perfectly and we made money on the deal. We had cash, the savings, the liquidity for me to take the time to get something substantial and not have to settle for a newspaper route."

In every job interview, Davis relived his time at Enron. "That was why I was a candidate; people knew that folks at Enron stood to know the industry pretty well. So, having to retell it over and over, there was probably some healing in that. I just had to get over it. I did pray during that time: I can't be bitter about this; I can't be nasty about this and still come off as professional. I knew that. Those things, yes, I turned to God for. Those were things that were least in my character. I was going to need help not being an ass."

Davis continues to this day to feel proud of the time he spent at Enron. "I was bold about it. I am still bold. I am not ashamed that I went there, the role that I played, and the folks that I worked with. I wouldn't defend what became of the people that were making nefarious decisions. But I wasn't ashamed of, in my mind, my spouse and those I worked closely with. We were just as much a victim as others. So I didn't have any issues with telling people, 'Yes, I lost everything.' Might as well put it out there; I didn't try to hide it from anybody. I wasn't ashamed of it. In some ways, I was proud of what we were doing. I thought it was pretty cool stuff."

It took a little while, but Davis landed a job with General Electric (GE). After EES went bankrupt, GE recognized there was an opportunity in what was left behind. Davis was the ideal candidate to make it happen. "While at GE, they hired me with the thought that they were going to try to make something on the mess that was left behind by Enron. We would go out to those customers. So I got hired as an industry specialist to help put something like that back together for them. Myself and a couple of other Enron guys got picked up."

Immediately Davis became acutely aware of the differences between Enron and GE. "The thing that was so different, GE had strict processes, procedures, controls, in place. There was no rogue anything. . .Enron was constantly trying to reinvent the wheel and we were encouraged to do so. Think out of the box, which was wonderful from an academic perspective, but not reality. Customers don't buy off the wall out of the box, as a rule."

He saw the value in getting to market smarter, not faster. "Enron's model was not to be exact. If you missed your ROI by two or three months on the calculation side, you could probably make it up with speed. How fast you could get those projects installed, that was much more critical than being 100 percent accurate on your project costs—

much more money at stake. They were the epitome of 'time is money,' whereas at GE, that wasn't the case. At GE, managing your costs, managing the project, estimating it correctly, that was how the money was made, on the front end. Getting it right."

It became evident to GE that the Enron business model could not be duplicated within their environment. They recognized it to be the customer's responsibility to pay for upgrading their system. "If the customer didn't want to buy a lighting project because of the savings that it generated for them, ehh, on to the next one. So that was very different. It was nice for me to see, just for my own edification and professional growth, that those value propositions and revenue models that Enron was wagging around, while they were sexy, they weren't real. So it was good for me to learn that, or to see when it's done right what it looks like, early enough in my professional career to not be tainted."

Davis never got over getting burned by Enron, and while his new life was stable, he felt vulnerable. GE was not realizing the growth they had anticipated and Davis began to feel very uncertain of his future there. "I was there for just shy of about a year and I just couldn't get into it. I found myself really distrusting the notion that some talking head, who knows where, was making decisions that impacted my life personally, and fast. So I left."

Davis was offered an opportunity to buy fifty percent interest in an existing general contracting company. He brought with him the valuable lessons he learned at both Enron and GE. "I found myself behaving a lot more like GE, than Enron. And even to this day, in the sense that, you let people understand how to get something built and what it costs to get something built. Those are the talents that you need for putting together a value proposition on a job, or a project. You don't bring on some Wall Street whiz-bang to tell you how to price a lighting retrofit job. Use the proper skill sets or the proper experience for the tasks or deliverable at hand."

USING EVERY EXPERIENCE

Davis felt he needed to get out of the energy industry altogether and discovered it almost therapeutic when he switched to working in construction. "I found that it was also good for me to be doing something that wasn't associated with that whole Enron thing for a period of time. . .I wasn't having to process it over and over. You let it go. It was done. Nothing I could do."

Working as a business owner for six years allowed him the opportunity to call the shots but also feel the full impact, positive and negative, of his business decisions. In the end he ended up losing around $150,000, but the experience was invaluable. "I think that was where I decided that there were some limits to my entrepreneurial spirit. Mainly I really wanted a team around me. It wasn't going to be all on me. One of the things I have determined, with Pacific it was all on me. . .What I learned from that, I don't want to be that 'all on me' guy. There are just too many skill sets you have to be a master at."

Davis has finally found his dream job. "Where I am today, is very much a start-up environment, but there is a team of us and I'm perfectly comfortable with it. I only need to be good at the things that I know I am good at. Not all the other stuff too. That is nice."

REALIZING PERSONAL GROWTH

The time spent at Enron and the end experience was crucial in making Davis the successful professional he is today. "I think it definitely made me a more savvy businessman. Obviously, the whole blind faith in management, that wasn't going to cut it for me anymore. No way in hell. Which I probably needed to stop. I grew up professionally. . .I think I also became much more, by necessity, self-sufficient."

He has a deeper appreciation that what he does for a living is not the same as who he is. "I guess similarly, I had to learn that, 'Hey, who I am on that business card, that doesn't define me.' If I improved as a person at all, it was that maturity. I would like to think that I am not a different person, just more mature."

As a teenager, Davis witnessed his father lose everything when the bike shop he opened went bankrupt. "There were no jobs at the time; this was the mid-to-late 1970s. So nobody was hiring even though he had these really marketable skills. Nobody needed them at the time. . .He never whined or complained about it. I remember it was obvious that we had been impacted significantly in our lifestyle."

He saw that action was required in order to move forward and on. "I never saw him not get up in the morning and go to work, nor bitch about whatever it was that he did at work. I think from my perspective, perhaps reflecting, I never thought about it much at the time, but it never occurred to me that I was done in, that this was the end. Oh my gosh, he lost a house and a business, and he managed to bounce back. . .It was the work ethic that got him through. Put your head down and work hard: Things will happen. That's what I got from him, work ethic; it just wasn't acceptable not to keep trying,"

Davis firmly believes that prayer combined with action is the winning formula for getting through those tough times. "I think that work ethic that has to be what gets people through. The spiritual side is wonderful; I am all for that. I have been teaching Sunday school for twenty years. I am all for that, but I think —pray like it depends on God; work like it depends on you. He gave us these skills, the mind and the hands. If we really have faith in Him and believe that everything about our existence is a gift, isn't it heretical not to keep using it, not to trust in it, which is not to trust in what He gave us?"

A WORD OF ADVICE

Continually investigate ways to stay current within your profession. "People have to be vigilant about being marketable. You have to constantly be learning. Whether it is as a specialist or a generalist, you just can't go stale."

Find inner value outside of work. "Whether somebody has a theological faith-based life or not, you have to have something that is not just work. You can't be your job. Whether it's with interests, or family, or it's a faith thing, you can't just identify yourself with your business card; that's temporary. I think that was the big thing for me, was how it just kind of humbled me."

FOR THOSE FACING A LAYOFF

Use this experience to bring about positive change.
"I think it is very important that people move on. Take these lumps, build some calluses, and get on with your life. Make something good out of it. It's out there. You can make good from these kinds of experiences."

Push through the pain. "You do need to mourn and process, but you can't be paralyzed by that; it can't consume you."

Set the example for your children. "Especially as a father with two daughters, one of things that was immediately, by the grace of God, high on my mind, was being the example of a man, a husband, a father to my daughters, going through a tough time. How I handled that, I needed to be a role model. It was important to me."

Prayer is not a replacement for action. "I have never been comfortable in leaning on God, like for provision or what have you, feeling like God owed me that. It's up to me, I have always felt. I would pray for the strength, I would pray for the patience, I would pray for the attributes that would make it easier."

"Life belongs to the living, and he who lives must be prepared for changes."

-Johann Wolfgang von Goethe

COLIN BAILEY

LONDON, ENGLAND – 1 YEAR 4 MONTHS

Colin Bailey was excelling in his field, and that was precisely why Enron wanted him. "I was approached by Enron. I was working for a big investment bank in Canary Wharf, and I had just got a promotion. I got a call from a senior finance director. I called her back and we had a long chat."

Enron was not a company he knew much about. Bailey needed the stability of a steady job and he wasn't about to leave for a new company without doing some homework. "I made a few calls. I knew a senior director at Enron, whom I'd worked with before. Everyone said to me, Enron is the place to work. It was perceived in London as this huge organization that had done so well and was going places."

With the recommendation of everyone he spoke to, Bailey thought this company ought to be taken seriously. "The following week they were in Canary Wharf meeting me for lunch; by the end, they were making me an offer. It sort of gave me an opportunity to go into a position, where at that point in time I might not be ready for it, but what they threw at me I couldn't refuse. You could write your own salary. I got a sign-on bonus to compensate for any bonus that I would lose by leaving."

With great confidence he signed on with Enron. "At the time it sort of looked too good to be true; it was a hell of an opportunity. . .I went along, I got a good feel, I thought this was something I couldn't refuse. There was travel as well to Houston; there was a global team based there. It was sort of a big opportunity for me."

A REASON TO TAKE RISKS

Bailey needed the money. His daughter Matilda, 'Tilly', has been battling a rare disease since she was six months old and the costs to support his daughter were mounting. Most recently her life hung in balance as a result of an infection in her feeding tube. The infection had spread throughout her body and her long-term prognosis was grim.

On two separate occasions the Bailey family was asked to consider switching off the life support machine. They could not. An expert on rheumatology reviewed her chart and suspected a rare auto-inflammatory disorder known as Chronic Infantile Neurological Cutaneous and Articular (CINCA) syndrome, also referred to as NOMID (Neonatal Onset Multisystemic Inflammatory Disease). The doctor suggested a steroid treatment to reduce the inflammation. It worked, and six months later Tilly returned home. Although they were able to successfully treat the symptoms, she requires regular ongoing treatment.

Tilly fought back each time the odds were stacked against her. As any father would, Bailey wanted to be able to give her every opportunity to excel. Unfortunately, Tilly doesn't qualify for medical insurance. Whenever treatment is needed, the Bailey family must raise the funds.

The job at Enron seemed like a dream come true. Bailey imagined being able to afford any treatment necessary to help his very sick daughter and support his family without having to make hard decisions. "When I joined. . .you could buy ten percent of your salary in shares, and if you bought ten percent, they doubled it. You could put your bonus in, and they'd double it. . .I know a lot of people who did that. They were encouraged to do it. On the website, on the internet, there was actually a page that was very open showing you the sales of Enron shares and the money that was made by senior executives, and it was absolutely astronomical."

Based on what he was seeing, people were making serious money with Enron stock. He opted to gamble and bought as much stock as he could. "I remember sitting in the first day thinking '$82 a share'. . .thinking in five years' time I could pay my mortgage off, thinking 'This is the place to be.'"

NO PLACE LIKE ENRON

Working at Enron was unlike working at any other employer. Bailey had always worked in the investment banking world. His last company was notoriously the strictest in London. He had never seen many unnecessary expenditures as he saw at Enron. "Everyone had an iPAQ at the time. . .It was pretty easy for someone to sign up to get one. Everybody had laptops. Traders initially got Red Bull as a drink in the kitchenettes on the floors. And then, all of a sudden every other floor had it. And they were spending over $120,000 a year on Red Bull alone. It was obscene."

After traveling to Houston he was astounded with the sheer amount of money being spent on everything. "I remember walking into the new building that was being fitted out, that linked to the old building, and it was a skywalk, it was like something out of *Star Wars*. I remember walking into the trading floor with the CIO and seeing more technology and more money spent than I have ever seen in my entire life. I am not joking. I had never seen so many plasma screens; it was like a plasma screen per desk. . .The money and how vast it was, I was like, 'My God, are we really generating enough money to pay for this AND the upkeep?' It was amazing."

Bailey ran the European Procurement Function. He didn't realize it at the time, but a team of individuals from Houston brought it upon themselves to try and take over the European team he was on. He was appalled at the way money was being thrown at him and his team. "I remember going over and being taken out to dinner. I was actually really shocked, alarmed, that I was taken to an incredible steak house, where I had never seen such expensive steaks, expensive drinks. And we were there to save money. And you didn't have two or three people turning up to this meal; you had fifteen to twenty people from the team turning up. I walked away and said to my boss, 'This isn't right, this was obscene, this is mad.'"

Looking back, it was obvious what their motives were. It rubbed him the wrong way. "The front office saw to it to butter us all up and get in control of us, and I just didn't like it at all. I found it really strange. Every day I got offers to be taken out to lunch to different restaurants. And we were in a money-saving department, not a money-making department. So the whole attitude at Enron was 'They don't care; we can do what we want.' And they got away with it. It was rotten."

It didn't take long before Bailey saw some real problems at Enron. "I was doing big deals with some big organizations and I tried to do some reciprocal trading. So we were buying off these companies, and I tried to get Enron in front of British Airways (BA) to hedge fuel. The hedge fuel guy never returned the calls. Now I am looking at multimillion-pound deals on a reciprocal trade. Unbeknownst to me they tried to do that with BA in years past and mucked up on the deal and ended up owing BA a lot of money."

Unfortunately this was not a rare occurrence. He began to see a pattern develop and he wondered how they were even making any money with their half-cocked approach to business. "They were way out of their league. I got the impression that Enron would try to get in something, create a market, and if there was potential throw a lot of money at it without knowing the full implications or the infrastructure that was needed."

WATCHING IT ALL FALL APART

Bailey was working hard during his time at Enron, and senior leadership recognized him for a promotion. Unfortunately, just before that was to happen he lost his job. "I was to be made director. I was going to get a big pay raise; I was going to get a thirty percent bonus."

On November 9, 2001, it was announced that Dynegy would buy Enron for a reported $9.5 billion. Everyone working for Enron held out hope that the deal would come through and their jobs would be saved. On November 28, Enron's credit rating was downgraded to junk status and the anticipated acquisition fell through. "I remember being on the trading floor, standing next to a very senior person. . .and Enron got turned to junk status—which meant, that was it."

Bailey was in shock at what he was witnessing. "All the traders stood up, starting shaking each other's hands. . . The guy next to me, who was a very senior guy, shook my hand and said, 'You never gave up until the end trying to save us money.'"

It was difficult for Bailey to fully grasp the gravity of the situation. All he really knew was that everything he had worked for was gone. "On that day the share price was suspended at sixty cents, something like that. Sixteen months prior, I had joined at $82. There were all these expectations, all these people telling me, 'This is the place to work, they are going to be like a Coca-Cola, lots of different markets,' to sixteen months later with the share price suspended at 60 cents, trying to understand what really was happening. I had never been in that situation."

More than 1400 people worked for Enron Europe in London. On Friday, November 30, Bailey was among the 1100 employees laid off. "I remember on the last day, I was sort of panicked, sort of, 'What I am going to do?' We got told on two different floors by PwC, the administrators, basically what was going on. What they were doing is keeping a skeleton staff to help them with winding Enron down."

Bailey knew before the formal announcement was made that he too would be losing his job that day. "I was told by my boss I wasn't going to be part of that because of my salary. . .he made his decision because I wasn't going to be able to help with the bankruptcy."

Inside, he felt robbed. He understood the reasons behind being let go; it made perfect business sense. The unfortunate part was losing out on the voluntary redundancy program Enron had offered its employees a few months prior to the layoffs in an attempt to cut costs. "I was going to get a great bit of money, but my boss couldn't let me go at that time."

Bailey and some co-workers grabbed a beer from the corner pub and watched the chaos unfold. "I remember standing outside the building watching BBC reporters trying to coax people into vehicles, where they are filming, to talk to them in tears. I remember recruitment consultants handing out cards. . .I remember people walking out in bits."

He met up later with a recruiter and another co-worker at a nearby wine bar. "We stood there with a glass of champagne and toasted each other and said, 'Good luck!' I walked out and I am like, 'Oh, what am I going to do? I've got Christmas, I've got a child. . .It was a very horrible feeling."

HOLDING ON TO WHAT MATTERS MOST

It was almost more than Bailey could bear. The $20,000 he had invested in Enron was gone. He had thought he was making the best decision for his family; now they were worse off than before. "It's like, 'I've got nothing. I've lost all my savings. I thought I was doing the right thing with something that looked incredible, and I've lost it all'. . . I couldn't pay December's mortgage because all my savings was gone. What do I do? We have to put payments off. It was like the world has fallen out beneath you."

He went home and looked at his family and determined that as long as they were healthy, nothing else mattered. "But with what we had been through the year before, we were like, it was only money, it is material. . .It put it in perspective for me. Being through what we've been through with my daughter, how she was on life support with septicemia a year before, it was like, 'Well, come on, there are a lot more important things. It's a job, it's money; there are jobs out there. We will get something.'"

Bailey had talked to some friends in Houston and felt his losses were nothing compared to some of theirs. He was barely 30 years old; they were much closer to retirement and had little time to rebuild what was lost. "But if you lived in Houston, gave your life to Enron, worked there all those years and put money in the pension, you are facing—what are you facing? I just thought, there is always someone worse off, and this is life and you've got to get on with it. No one is going to do it for you. You've got to get on with it."

Fortunately, his mortgage company understood completely and gave him some time to find a job and get back on his feet. "It was obviously very publicized. There was some sympathy for it: 'We will give you some breathing space.' There was still pressure to find something, but there was some understanding, which was helpful. If you contact these companies, they'll listen; they aren't going to throw you out. If you don't contact them, then obviously you are asking for trouble. Luckily we did that."

Bailey hit the streets everyday looking for a job. More than his life depended upon it. "I spent the next six weeks non-stop, looking for work, which is Christmas period, which isn't the easiest. I was very lucky to find a position six weeks later in a global investment bank. I worked in a bar part-time, for socializing, for a little petrol money, and networking again. I was doing everything I could to get another job. I was lucky to find one."

REFLECTING UPON THE ENTIRE EXPERIENCE

Bailey accepts he did the best he could with the information given to him. "Things never really added up, they never did, and yet I kept putting in the shares, still kept dreaming, like a lot of people did. . .It wasn't encouraged. I just kept doing it. I was asking questions, but everyone thought that it would turn itself around. Nobody really realized the depth of what had happened: that was the problem."

When the CEO of Enron, Jeffrey Skilling, came to London, Bailey could not believe how that meeting was conducted. "I remember going to a talk by Skilling. He came over and he gave a talk up in the conference center. . .They used to get 50-odd pizzas from Pizza Hut just to encourage you to go and listen to what the business was doing and how they have increased profits by thirty percent on a quarterly basis. People would turn up for the pizza! I thought, 'What kind of gimmick is this?'"

He now sees the true character of his former leader. "When Skilling came over, I must admit, I thought he was a straight guy. He was impressive. A bit like Clinton versus Bush; he knew the business and he talked it well. But yet this air that no one would challenge him. Then later on seeing what happened to the business, and how he was and how he reacted to the analysts who challenged him, I thought, you are more Bush than Clinton—like a bull in a china shop."

Bailey applauds Enron on how they empowered people to do their best and looked into all possibilities. "They tried to create markets, and they tried to look at radical ideas. It is possible it is what brought them down. On the other side, I used to look at radical ideas to save money, and they would listen to them, and at times try them."

He still remembers walking into the reception area to see a brand new BMW sports car on display. To save money on recruitment costs, Enron asked its employees to recommend people they knew to join the ranks of Enron. If that person was hired, the employee's name was entered into a drawing for the sports car at the end of the year. "I thought that was very innovative. They saved probably half a million by the amount of people who were recommended that came into the business, and they were giving away probably a $30,000 car. . .They would look at the radical, so from that perspective that is what made them interesting, but on the other side, that is what brought them down."

Overall the entire experience has had a positive influence on Bailey's life. "I would say that has been more positive than negative: The fact that I have gone to work for some of the biggest organizations in the world *after* that, and people see that and show me a bit of respect for that. If I was part of the wrongdoing, I wouldn't have been going on to work for some of the top organizations in the world."

A WORD OF ADVICE

Keep a watchful eye to the signs. "Where a company can't justify its existence, where a company starts hiding things and you start to hear things."

Know as much as possible about the company. "I make myself busy within businesses if I am not sure of that business to try and understand it more. Because I am not in the moneymaking areas, I am in cost-cutting; I am in saving money. So, it's easy to get a job in these businesses to go in and save money, but I like to understand more about how they are making money now."

If questions arise, look outside the company for answers. "I ask around for people that know what they are talking about, whereas, at Enron, I was just asking people who were in the business and they are all tied up the same as me. Even people in moneymaking areas didn't see what was coming, even though they might say that now. They were hoping they weren't going to lose what they'd invested, and it was a gambler's mentality I would say—they knew you were going to lose it, but they were going to hope that you wouldn't."

Consider the risks and rewards before investing. "I used to do penny shares and things. I calmed down a lot of that, because all I saw at Enron, the promotion, the 'buy one get one free,' the \$82 share, and got sold on it, it was a bit brainwashing. I feel I am a lot more savvy now. If I am going to make an investment, I am going to do it for the right reasons and I am going to look at the potential risks a lot more now."

No such thing as a sure thing. "Nothing in life is a surety. You can know the trainer, the horse and the down-and-dirty details, but in the end there is no guarantee of a win."

There is too much of a good thing. "The lack of control was scary. It attracted greed. When you get more you want more. Flexibility is good but the business must make enough money to pay for it."

FOR THOSE FACING A LAYOFF

Keep the focus on moving forward. "You have to move on. If I run into anyone who is bitter or angry about past experiences, I just move on. You can't get wrapped up in that stuff. You have to focus on the positive; you have to focus on doing bigger and better things."

To learn more about Matilda 'Tilly' Bailey or to make a donation, please visit: http://www.TillysAppealFund.com

"Far and away the best prize that life has to offer is the chance to work hard at work worth doing."

-Theodore Roosevelt

LEONCIO FLORES

HOUSTON, TEXAS – 11 MONTHS

*L*eoncio Flores was working as programmer for an IT consulting company when the opportunity to work for Enron opened up. He had heard people saying this was the place to be if you wanted to make a lot of money quickly. "My boss said, 'All the guys are moving over to Enron.' This was in early 2000. Fortune 7 company, they have stock shares, you get a free laptop or desktop, you get all these perks. I got interested in earning more money, and it came true when I joined Enron."

Immediately after starting at Enron, Flores knew this was not the working environment he was used to. At previous jobs he felt like an employee; at Enron he felt like family. "My first week at Enron, it was so nice; everyone was so friendly. Friendly in the way of, 'Hey, Leo, are you in need of any technical books? I have some I can lend to you, no strings attached.' Things like that. Even my boss was so nice. It was kind of strange, not like other companies, where you are just a name or a number. It was a different environment: 'You are one of us.'"

Flores and his group willingly gave every project the best they had to give. "First, what I really love about Enron,

everybody wanted to do something better than it was.
. .Since I was doing software development, it was really
good. The latest methodologies we are practicing, everyone is thorough in terms of detail. We have the thinking
that we should excel. . .We are really practicing, and we are
calling it 'The Enron Way.'"

NO PLACE LIKE ENRON

Enron recognized talent and it wasn't long before Flores
was invited to move up. "I was promoted to project
manager in three months. I was pushed to the limit; I
pushed myself to the limit. . .I was working years for so
many companies and I never got promoted that fast. Here
I am at Enron and someone noticed how good I am and
gave me more challenges; I loved it."

The opportunity lit his entrepreneurial spirit and allowed
him the opportunity to feel the highs and lows of starting
a new venture but without the personal risk. "It was like
starting a new company within a company. That department was just starting up. . .I had to build up my team
and hire people from outside or maybe from within, so
it was nice. It was a recognition I had never experienced
anywhere."

There were no rules of etiquette when it came to meetings
at Enron. "I loved it when they would say, 'Okay, we have a
small meeting, come with me we'll go to Starbucks down-
stairs or go have some coffee.' We could meet anywhere,
that's one thing. We could talk shop while eating and it's
not going to bother me; as if every moment counted."

People who worked at Enron felt so passionately about
their jobs that heated arguments often erupted. In the

end everyone worked together because they were working towards the same goal. "Of course we'd argue over issues, but not relational issues, not too very personal. There were disagreements, we agreed to disagree kind of thing, but it was all about work because we wanted to make things better."

Flores recounts one especially memorable argument in his department. "Two managers, right in the middle of a meeting, were really arguing, really heated. Nothing personal, just the difficult things you see and hear in a heated meeting. After they finished arguing, one of them asked, 'Okay, we are having lunch now; are you paying or do I?'"

Both parties calmed and it was as if nothing had happened. One said, "Oh, wait, it is my turn now. Okay, let's go down and have lunch."

"It was just like that. That was how they respected each other. Me, coming from Filipino-Asia and who used to live in Saudi Arabia for eleven years, it was very rare for people to argue so much."

THE DARK CLOUDS FORM

Enron began to change during the last few months of 2001 and people inside were beginning to talk. Flores heard the rumors and he saw the news but he wasn't sure what to think. "I think it was mid-November when we started to become news. I asked my director and my senior manager about it and they said, 'We will go over the edge and that's it. If not, we will hurdle this hump and we will still be Enron, the best of the best.'"

Flores felt some concern and made a half-hearted attempt to find another job. He didn't want another job. He wanted

Enron to survive. But he knew he needed to have options because he had a family to support. "People were sending out emails saying here is this headhunter who is a friend of mine, if you have a résumé forward it to him or her. . .When the emails are spreading around, headhunters and all these things, I joined the craze. I sent emails, I had interviews, you know, to get ready for this."

His résumé was selected and Flores was invited to come in for an interview. "I was applying with an IT consulting company somewhere in downtown Houston. I was there for an interview and there was a long line of fifteen or twenty men and women and they were all from Enron. All of us."

He realized he wasn't the only one concerned about losing his job at Enron. He had never seen so many people waiting for an interview. It shocked him and he went back to thinking that maybe Enron would recover and he would never have to look for another job again.

It was business as usual in his department and little was done to prepare them for the shock of being laid off. "We were joking with each other until the very last week. We were throwing paper at each other; there was laughing. But everyone was so disillusioned on the last day. When the news came out, that's when it was like the *Titanic* was sinking."

SAYING GOODBYE TO ENRON

The gravity of the situation finally hit Flores and his team. "It was a very, very, sad experience. . .All my friends were just staring at their monitors. We were kind of sad. We had been sad for the last week before it happened. I was in an early denial stage; I can't accept the fact it will collapse. . . It was emotionally difficult. I can't sleep at night; the television news, I change channels. I don't want to hear the news, because I work at Enron, so I don't need to know the news."

It broke his heart to leave the job he loved. "I was sad, angry, that day when it happened. I had a bag with me to take technical books from my office. I didn't take anything Enron; I don't like keeping that memory. It really hurts. In November when Enron was in the local news, my wife was cutting out all the headline news about Enron, and when we left, I threw it all away. I had come to hate Enron. I had even collections of things but I left them. I don't want to work again and remember I was in heaven and now I have been thrown out of heaven."

On Monday, December 3, everyone was gathered into a meeting and told their fate. Flores and his group could hardly contain their emotions as the words they most feared were finally said: "The company has collapsed. Get your bags ready and packed up and take them when you leave."

For the first time in his life Flores openly cried. As the memories of that fateful day return, Flores is surprised to find it still affects him. "My manager and others, we all cried. Nice memories, really nice memories. That last day, we just can't stop crying, and I am a man who never cries. I hate crying; I feel ashamed if people see my eyes. I think it was the first time in my whole life I really cried in front of men, and they were crying in front of me. . .I have the box still from that day and I haven't opened it. It was really hard. Wow, it's been a long time and I can really feel it."

FINDING A NEW SPONSOR

Flores was working legally in the United States using an HiB working visa. This special visa cannot be obtained by the immigrant, only by the sponsoring employer. It is a temporary work visa granted to immigrants with specialized, professional skills. This visa is not permanent and is revocable if the immigrant loses his or her sponsor and is unable to secure new employment. "So when it happened, I said, 'INS said if I don't have a job after two weeks, we will have to leave America.'"

For the next few weeks Flores applied for as many jobs as he could. With his qualifications and experience he received many invitations to interview. Unfortunately the employment pool was saturated with many other displaced Enron employees and he was never able to find another job. "I go in an interview, always there is a line of people. . .And there are ten or twenty Enron guys in there, all wearing dark suits. I have only with me a five-page résumé printed out on a piece of paper. And the guys ahead of me have folders of portfolios; they have their diplomas. Wow, they're ready for a presentation!"

Although he was a dedicated and talented employee for Enron, so was everyone else. He found himself unable to compete against the crowd. "I saw one guy, his diploma was from UCLA, another I think was from University of Miami, all of them universities. Here I am; I have a degree from a university in the Philippines that nobody knew in America. Interviewer asked, 'Where did you take your MBA?' I say, 'Florida State University.' So all of them are graduates of big universities, top-of-the-line universities, standing in line, vying for the same position and I require a visa to stay and work in the U.S.. . .It was really discouraging. There were so many people to choose from."

THE FINANCIAL IMPACT

Flores and his family lived paycheck to paycheck and along with government assistance had barely enough to get by. "We didn't have any savings; we didn't prepare for that. I did get welfare. I just had enough; that I know."

Signing up for unemployment and welfare was a blow to Flores' ego. "It really feels so terrible emotionally because, even though I grew up in a poor country, in the Philippines, I never relied on others for money. I firmly believe that you must earn your keep and be generous in giving. I always hated people begging and I felt bad that now I have to beg for money to survive. It was the worst of times."

When he was hired, Flores took advantage of the many incentives offered to new employees. "Yes, everything was lost. I think $18,000 U.S. dollars in shares, stock options, and I bought a lot of Enron stock when I first started. I also lost my 401(k) from my previous company and all the money that I saved, retirement pay, all the money was in Enron stock. . .I lost around $25,000 to $30,000 in U.S. dollars."

Christmas was just around the corner and Flores and his family had to make some tough decisions. "We did not buy presents during Christmas because Enron collapsed and all of a sudden we do not want to put up the Christmas decorations anymore. The salary that I got at the end of November was supposed to buy some presents. It was hard to explain to my two daughters the economics of not buying a $20 present which we will use instead to buy groceries or pay for rent and utilities. The kids knew Santa is fictional but they loved the fact that gift-giving from Santa is seasonal fun, and they felt bad not to have lots of presents for the first time."

SEEING THE AMERICAN SPIRIT

When he returned home that night, he had never felt so desolate. His focus was on finding a new job, but there was little to help with the immediate needs of his family. During this dark moment in his life the brightness of the American spirit shone through. "So here I see people coming to my house after Enron; they knew my address and they came."

They lived in the same complex but he didn't know them very well. Now they were standing on his doorstep with a gift so generous he could hardly believe it. "They say, 'We have some money and if anything you need, you just call us.'" The group had gone out to their friends and neighbors to gather up as much as they could for Flores and his family.

Puzzled, he immediately questioned their motives. "I say, 'What is this? What's in it for you?'"

His questions were greeted with a smile and a reassurance that they had no ulterior motives. "They say, 'No, I just know that you were laid off. . .I had been laid off twice before, so we all know what you are going through.'"

This selfless act showed Flores why America is such a special place to live beyond the career opportunities. It is the people who go out of their way to help a hurting soul with no expectation of receiving anything in return. He now knew first-hand what it meant to be an American. "That was just a one-time thing. It's the great state of Texas. They really gave us hospitality; it was strange. I have never seen this before."

Numerous acts of kindness continued. He would find various food items on his doorstep, and once a stranger gave him a few dollars to take his children out for video games. It deeply touched him to be the recipient of such thoughtfulness during his time of need. "So, it's like people gathering to help. . .They know you are from Enron. 'We can bring you some cookies on Saturday. We're not rich but we have some extra cookies. If you want them I will send our boy on his bike over to your house.' Those small kinds of things."

FIGHTING IGNORANCE

To this day Flores has immense respect for America and its citizens. Whenever he can, he tells others about what he experienced. "I have been around. I've been over to Italy, other places, Canada, Mexico and even Europe. It's only at that time and that place that I have seen that kind of generosity expressed so much. Then I say, 'Wait, it is just like that in America wherever you go! It is just not the same in every country. When there is a disaster and people need help, they don't care what great thing you've done, they just help.'"

It amazes him when he travels internationally how poorly other countries treat American citizens. "I think I was in Belgium or in Denmark, there was some situation and they saw me, it was a tourist type of situation, they took me out of line and got me out of line first to be taken care of. You know who was the last in line after they checked in the people? The one with the American passport. Not everywhere, but. . .that kind of bigotry ran just about everywhere."

Flores believes it is because many do not know that Americans unselfishly give to those in need. "The good news is not being known. They don't know about the cakes that were sent to my house because they knew I was one of those Enron guys, the ex-Enron employee who lost everything. . .we are all broke now. . .It was really, a very nice experience. I have never experienced that kind of thing again."

RETURNING TO THE PHILIPPINES

Adding to the misery of unemployment was the concern for his child who became ill right after he was laid off. "During that time before Christmas my youngest daughter was sick. It was December 26 when she got well. We didn't even go out for Christmas, nothing; we tried to save money. I told them on December 28 that we would just go back to the Philippines."

With no job offers in sight and the threat of INS looming, it was suggested to Flores that he might have better luck returning to the Philippines and starting a software development company. "During that time when I was in the U.S., every job they are all going abroad, to places like China and India. It was cheaper labor. Someone said, 'You could go back to Philippines and start your own company.'"

To the average person, this might sound like an easy decision to make. To Flores and his family, it meant facing the ghosts of their past and forgiving a country that had threatened to wipe them out. "During the 1970s the Philippines was under the leadership of a dictator named Ferdinand Marcos. He made fake events, like assassination attempts and chaos, that prompted him to declare a fake martial law. Marcos then controlled the Philippines until 1986 when he was thrown out by people power. We grew up knowing the terrible corruption and I was an activist together with my family. The reprisal was terrible.

They would arrest people and then they just disappeared. My father was kidnapped and we just found him dead and placed in a basket with obvious torture marks. We were forced to arm ourselves for protection, change homes and eventually leave the country."

They were filled with trepidation as they prepared to leave for the Philippines. "It was really something. Wow, go back home again after so many years outside of the country, a little bit of a difficult adjustment. My children and my wife, they all cried, we all cried. It was the toughest."

A CHANGED MAN

Returning home turned out to be the best thing for Flores and his family. The entire experience caused him to trust more in God and His plan. "When that happened, everything worked out well. God answered my prayer to give me a job, make things better."

He formed his own consulting company Uy & Flores Consulting (www.uyflores.com). "When I went back to the Philippines on January 28, 2002 to establish my own firm, I immediately got a client. I flew to Brussels, Belgium in March for a one-month project. The Enron experience gave me great knowledge in becoming a better manager."

He also became somewhat of a business celebrity in the Philippines teaching SWOT-RICE courses (Strengths, Weaknesses, Opportunities and Threats, with the add-on of Respect, Integrity, Communication and Excellence). "One thing that Enron helped me in was to train people. They emphasized a lot of training."

Flores took that training and began teaching other companies about this SWOT-RICE, known as, "The Enron

Way." "They were all surprised. They would say, 'Wow, this is a great thing to hear!' I never gave credit to Enron. . .I now teach SWOT-RICE to just about everybody here in the Philippines who wants to have project management. I teach all my clients here and abroad SWOT-RICE, they accept it, and I am evangelistic. . . It makes people laugh because us Filipinos, we eat rice, so it's funny."

Eventually he had to walk away from teaching for more lucrative and stable opportunities. He sees it as just another option if he ever needs a job. "Now I have to turn down the teaching opportunities because I have a regular job. . .Now I am ready for a layoff. I got money ready, and I had to find ways to have another way to earn money. Like teaching, if things were to happen later on, it is something to fall back on. I can always go back to teaching."

In 2008 he learned just how ready he was when the job he had disappeared overnight. "Enron made me a very, very strong man. I got laid off recently. . .The U.S. economy went down and we were affected terribly. That very day, I and around 38 or 40 people in my department were laid off. In my department alone, there are almost 200 people laid off in one day here in the Philippines. . .I was prepared. I made friends with all the headhunters here in the Philippines and the U.S., and I am always in the loop with all of them. . .I sent them an email and they swarmed over me."

WORDS OF ADVICE

Be satisfied with who you are today. "Be content with who you are and what you are. . . I have always been content with what I have. I never was materialistic. When I joined Enron; it was nice to have all those material things that were free. After I lost everything, I learned to be content."

Combat fear with preparation. "Get ready for anything worse that could happen in life. The Enron thing, after that happened to me, I am now ready for anything that happens in life; I am not afraid to get laid off."

Diversify investments. "Spread the eggs in the nest; don't put them in one basket. I have mutual funds, not much, but they have high yields.. . .I still have American Treasury Bonds from back then. Now I am really prepared. Yes, financially I am ready; I have money ready."

Have a backup job. "I once wanted to buy a car that I could use. My thinking was I would buy a taxi that I would use as a service. So when I go to the office I could get paid, and if I get laid off I could be a full-time driver. That kind of thinking, that kind of mentality, that is what I learned after Enron."

FOR THOSE FACING A LAYOFF

There is no such thing as job security. "Have the mentality that those kinds of things will happen to just about anyone; everyone. I have a friend who worked eighteen years for IBM and then all of a sudden he got laid off from IBM. I have another friend who worked for HP and his whole life was HP, and all of a sudden in 2008 he was laid off. It is like that, you have to be ready to accept it."

Find something to hold on to. "Get ready to be strong emotionally; it's the most traumatic experience. If they have a family, family is the best way to go. If they are single, go and get your strength from God, from your church; you got to have to have someone to hang on to. It's difficult. It's like, 'Why was I laid off? Why was I the one chosen? I am better than this other guy.' It's really difficult."

"We define ourselves by the best that is in us, not the worst that has been done to us."

-Edward Lewis

JIM AND MARY LESSOR

HOUSTON, TEXAS

MARY – 21 YEARS, JIM – 11 YEARS

*M*ary started working for Enron first, when it was InterNorth, in 1980. "I worked for them until InterNorth bought Houston Natural Gas which became Enron. So in 1986, we moved from InterNorth in Omaha to Enron in Houston."

When news came that her job was moving to Houston, Mary was delighted to be offered a relocation package. "Even though I was in just an administrative type of job, I still felt valued. For InterNorth to pay for a secretary basically to move to Houston was amazing to me, because they could have hired someone off the street to do my job. But they offered me a job there and would buy our house, and sent us to look for a house down here."

Without hesitation Jim and Mary decided to take Enron up on its offer and move the family down to Houston. Jim remembers, "I was all for it, because I wanted to get out of the cold weather. I came down without a job and figured the long-term opportunities here were better in Houston."

Although Jim found a job, he jumped at the chance to be hired on at Enron. "I started as a contractor in October of 1990 and was hired full time by March of 1991, starting out doing reconciliations for the liquids group, and then I was promoted to an accounts payable supervisor after that."

NO PLACE LIKE ENRON

Mary remembers Enron as being a charitable organization. "They had this fundraiser and I gave money. If you participated you had a chance to win a BMW Z3. Lo and behold, my name was picked to be a part of that. They had this big dinner. Afterwards they had the people come up on stage whose names were drawn. Somebody had a bunch of keys in his hand. He went down the line and you picked a key. If your key started the car, it was yours. I didn't win, but that was fun."

Jim enjoyed the challenging work environment. "I was taken off my job and put on this huge reconciliation project because they had switched systems and the accounts were messed up. We had debit balances where we shouldn't have debit balances. . .I figured out what was wrong with the system, the programming, and why all the entries were wrong. I remember coming home and was very happy because I had finally figured out why we were off. . .That was my happiest moment at Enron."

In the mid-1990s a new performance-review process was introduced. Jim noticed how it changed the culture, making it a very competitive working environment where no job was secure. "It was known as the 'rank and yank' system, and what Skilling wanted was the bottom ten percent let go every year. You were constantly scrambling to make yourself look good," Jim explains.

In the back of his mind Jim felt uneasy with all the new changes, but in his position there was little he could do but watch. In hindsight he sees it clear as day. "It just was the way Skilling changed things: the Mark-to-Mark accounting he introduced, the change of actual physical delivery of product to the derivatives and all this other stuff. It precipitated, and I think hastened, the downfall. . . I just wished I would have acted upon the signs. I let my heart lead me instead of my brain."

BLINDSIDED

In late September, Kenneth Lay boasted to his employees that Enron stock was "an incredible bargain." Both Jim and Mary believed what Lay was telling them. Sensing an opportunity, they went ahead and purchased more stock. Jim says, "When Skilling left in August of 2001, Lay convinced us everything was hunky-dory. Mary and I bought extra stock in October of 2001."

Mary worked in the Human Resources Compensation department. From her vantage point, there were no signs indicating an imminent collapse. "I had no clue. Just that last week, the only thing that I remember is seeing was [an Enron executive] on our floor a lot, and usually she would say 'hi' and have a happy face. I know the week before the bomb dropped she was not happy; she looked really, really, worried to me. But I just thought maybe she was having a bad day. I didn't think what was about to happen."

Mary helped administrate the employee stock-option program. After the bankruptcy she knew she was out of a job. "What I remember is [another Enron Executive] was walking around carrying a Bible; I remember that. I also remember her calling us all into her office and she was crying. She said she had done all she could do, but she never told us who gets to stay and who's going to be terminated. I knew I would be, because of my job. At bankruptcy those things would be totally worthless, so I pretty much knew then."

In the midst of this highly emotional moment, it floored Mary when a co-worker began to boast about her potential retention. "One person in particular kind of bragged about the fact that because of her position, that they were going to keep her on. It bugged me that she had bragged about that under the circumstances."

Likewise, Jim was caught off guard. His job kept him busy up until the bankruptcy. "I came in to work that day and started doing my stuff and I thought, 'What was the use?' It came through that we had declared bankruptcy. All of us from the old building went over to the new building. We just hung around on the trading floor waiting to hear what happened. They put us together on the trading floor and said, 'Everybody go home, and you'll get a call from somebody later.' So I went back to the original building, packed up my stuff and went home."

The words left Jim feeling numb as he made his way back to his desk. How could this have happened? His mind raced as he gathered up his things. With no answers, he took one last look and left without a word. On his way out of the building he was captured on film by media crews. "Channel 11, a CBS station here, showed me coming out of Enron with my box. So I was on TV a lot of times."

Mary's fate was in limbo while she awaited confirmation of what she already suspected. "A couple of days later this guy called me. He didn't come right out and say; he kind of beat around the bush. I said, 'What are you telling me, am I terminated?'" To that the man responded, "Yep, yep, that is what I am telling you." It was finally over.

FINANCIAL IMPACT

They were only a few years from retirement when 75 percent of their retirement money disappeared. They know it is unlikely they will ever fully recover. Jim explains, "You have to understand that Mary and I were not like some 30-year-old guy who had been there three or four years. That to them was like a small blip on the radar screen of life; they could come back. Mary and I lost 32 years of combined retirement between us. So for the older people, I'm 59 years old and my wife was 60, it has been a hard time for a lot of us because we were older and lost a lot more than the younger people did."

For Jim, it's his worst nightmare come true. "One of my lifelong trepidations was to get to retirement and not have two dollars to buy a golf ball. Sure enough, my worst fears came through with Enron because I am probably going to have to continue working until I keel over at my desk."

Both were filled with bitterness and anxiety after the layoff. Four days later they found a reason to celebrate. "On December 7, I won five numbers in the lottery, and that allowed us to have a better Christmas."

Throughout the years various lawsuits have been filed and won for those who were laid off. Their settlement doesn't even come close to covering what they lost. "From all the Enron settlements that have gone on for the past ten years, we have collected a little less than $30,000 between us."

Today they are at peace with their situation and have chosen to focus on what they do have. Jim explains, "It is still not the end of the world. If we would have worked for a normal company like Exxon, we would be sitting pretty right now. It just didn't happen. Nothing we can do about it, can't change the past, just have to go forward and make the best out of each day."

MARY FINDS HER CALLING

Mary had dedicated her life to Enron and the entire fallout left her disenchanted. She knew she needed to find a job, but she had no interest in returning to anything similar to Enron. "I had some deaths in my immediate family, so I didn't look right away, but I did look. That whole thing sort of gave me a bad taste for big corporate America."

During the hiatus from working, she took some time to evaluate exactly what she wanted to do. "I felt it was time for a change. I had never worked in the retail world, and I wanted to give it a go. It wasn't hard to get a retail job; I have been doing that ever since."

Although the money isn't what she used to make, she enjoys all the other benefits which come with the job. "I got hired with a local department store. I am a little sales associate making less than half what I used to make. I like it because it is close to home; the hours are different, which allows me to do more things at home than I did when I worked eight to five."

Through her sales position, Mary discovered her love of selling. "It has allowed me to learn to sell. I learned I can sell on eBay; in fact that is one of my goals, to make a living doing that, because that's how much I like it. I would have never learned that if I was still working for Enron."

JIM RETURNS TO ENRON

When Jim was let go, he began searching for a new job, but soon found the market to be saturated with candidates. "I was looking right away. . .There were a lot of people let go all at one time. There's a lot of people all of a sudden in the market. Some potential employers wanted former Enron employees, and some wouldn't have anything to do with them; it just depended on what you were doing."

Although his position wasn't considered eligible for retention when bankruptcy occurred, it became evident later that it was indeed essential. "When I was gone for three months, nobody at Enron had done any collections. There was all this money owed to Enron sitting on the books, and finally they realized after three months, 'We'd better bring Jim back.' That was how I got hired back."

Jim felt any job was better than no job, and diligently went to work to accomplish what he had been hired to do. He never anticipated the emotional stress he would have to encounter. "Well, it was kind of eerie. I went back to my old floor. The main building was empty; the original Enron building was empty but the papers, everything, was still there. It was like a ghost town. . .One guy that I'd worked with ever since the beginning at Enron came back to work in the accounting area. . .He stayed there for thirty days but he just could not do it anymore. . .but I stuck it out."

Before the layoffs, Jim had derived great pride from a hard day's work. He willingly invested extra time and energy into ensuring his job was done correctly and as efficiently as possible. That all changed when he returned. "I brought in like $12 million for the estate, but I wasn't super-duper motivated like I was when Enron was alive. I figured, 'What the heck are they going to do?' The worst they could do was fire me. I would do my best to bring in all the money on the books while I was there. I didn't care about it as much."

As time went on he began to fully comprehend the reasons why Enron went down. He began to blame upper management for allowing it to occur in the first place. "I realized, how could this have happened? There was a lot of bitterness. . .I knew my job would eventually end when my job was done; which it did. When I collected all the money I could, that was it. . .I worked at Enron from March 2002 to June 2003."

JIM FINDS HIS MIRACLE

Finishing out his job at Enron allowed him to fully close that chapter of his life. When his last day came around, he felt immense relief. "I was happy when it ended in '03, because I was finally through with that place."

The whole experience drained Jim and he took time after Enron to find his dream job. "I started a car-detailing business in my garage. I was really, really bummed out and I wanted to get away from it for a while. . .I had some pretty dark days after Enron looking for a job."

It took some time but eventually he found a job. "When I got hired on at Apache we had $27 in our checking account. . .I got hired making about what I was making at Enron."

Immediately he noticed a very different working environment. "When I went to work for Apache, I almost had to retrain myself. You really had to stick up for yourself at Enron in order to survive. I had to change the way I interacted with people at Apache versus Enron because the culture was so different and I realized that only Enron was that way. . .it was a different place to work."

Unfortunately cutbacks were needed in his department and he was laid off again. "I worked there for two years until the economy took a downturn and our department went from four to one, and I was one of the ones they let go."

This time the layoff was less painful. "When I got laid off at Apache, we would have been in a world of hurt had they not given me such a fantastic severance package. They didn't really want to get rid of me, but they had no choice. I got a super, wonderful severance package, which allowed me time to look for a job."

Jim asked God to help him find the perfect job. "I prayed to God to help me get a job here in the Woodlands, with not so much stress, and let me go home at 5:00 p.m. every day, and that is exactly what I got. It was a miracle. . .I'm completely out of the energy industry; I'm completely out of oil and gas. I am in something completely new, less stressful, and the commute, it's just great. Don't have to drive but four miles to go into work."

CHANGED PEOPLE

Mary found the experience to affirm her trust in God and His plan. "I am a believer that things happen for a reason because we have something to learn. That Enron thing was apparently a part of my journey, and just to have faith in God that our journey will take us where we are supposed to be, that is how I look at it. Today, I am right where I am supposed to be."

She is completely contented with where she is today. "I am a lot closer to God. Unemployment teaches you patience, teaches that He is there for you when you think that nobody is. I am happy where I'm at today. It is not glamorous, I don't have a lot of money, but I am happy."

Jim has a new appreciation for the important things in life. "What I realized, for me, it was kind of like our own personal 9/11. . .If we can get through that, we can get through a lot of things. Other things that come up don't seem as big of a deal anymore. I've lived through other things. I've had a stay in the hospital in '05 where, what the heck, I could have died. You look at things differently after an experience like that."

WORDS OF ADVICE

Have a well-balanced investment plan. "Don't put all your eggs in one basket; diversify your retirement portfolio."

Past performance guarantees nothing. "Keep your eyes open for anything that may happen. I look back at things that I saw at Enron that I should have realized weren't exactly kosher, but the stock had been going up every year fifteen percent and I was just so blinded by the success I didn't stop and look at things more rationally."

Question authority. "Look out for huge changes, like Skilling brought in."

FOR THOSE FACING A LAYOFF

Layoffs can happen to anyone. "I've been there. It's not your fault. We didn't do anything wrong."

Look at the bright side. "Not the end of the world. You could look at it in a positive way that things turn out for the better."

Do what you can and have faith. "I know it is painful, but keep moving forward trying to do the best you can. God will be with you and it'll all work out."

" I have always argued that change becomes stressful and overwhelming only when you've lost any sense of the constancy of your life. You need firm ground to stand on. From there, you can deal with that change."

-Richard Nelson Bolles

PERRIN WORRELL

HOUSTON, TEXAS – 1 YEAR 6 MONTHS

*P*errin Worrell was a young and ambitious student at Baylor University. "In the business school, Enron was all anybody talked about. At Baylor it was Enron and Arthur Andersen; those were the two companies where everybody wanted to work."

Her mother and father were both teachers, so Worrell felt it was only natural to gravitate towards that degree. Even though education seemed a secure and promising career, she couldn't stop thinking about a conversation she had had with her grandfather. He advised her "to have plans A, B, C, D, E, F and G in place, if necessary."

The simple act of imparting an elder's life lesson ended up forever changing the way Worrell looked at any major decision. "I was in the School of Education, but I was getting a Computer Information Systems portion to my degree. I was trying to give myself a bunch of other outlets if I didn't want to do education and I could move on to something else."

After graduation Worrell returned home but found the job market soft for recent graduates. Everything changed when a friend called and wondered aloud if Worrell would be interested in moving with her to Houston. "I only had to think for one or two seconds and I said, 'I'm coming, I'll do it!'. . . I signed up with a temp agency who signed me up for a temp job at Enron."

OPPORTUNITY BY CHANCE

Worrell was more than excited about working for Enron, but the position was less than ideal. Undeterred, she checked in with the receptionist and began to wait to be called back. As she waited, a friend from college who was working at Enron happened to see Worrell sitting there. "She came through the lobby and said, 'Why are you here? There's a position that's come open that I think you would be perfect for. Let me go get my manager!'"

Worrell didn't realize it until later, but she shouldn't have been sitting there. A mistake had been made and she wasn't called back to her assigned temp job until after almost thirty minutes had passed. During that time she was able to informally interview for the job that would ultimately change her life. "So she went and got her manager and brought her out and we sat and talked for a little while and I said, 'This sounds great; I would love this!'"

Two weeks later she officially interviewed and was hired to work for Enron Network Services in the Recruitment Division of the Human Resources Department. Worrell immediately felt like a member of the group. "The great thing was that Enron was a giant family; even if you didn't like each other, you pretended you liked each other. It was an open environment; I could see across the entire room to the people on the other side. . . It was very open and the people were really nice."

She worked harder than she ever had in her life. "It was very stressful. I probably worked ten to twelve hours a day when I started. That was normal because Enron was still ramping up. That was the year they started Enron Energy Services and they built a couple of new companies right as I was getting on, so recruiting was going full force."

When Worrell was hired, there was a different human resources department for each company Enron had created. Four months later Enron decided to merge them. She had to re-interview and afterwards was assigned a more advanced position. Worrell soon discovered she wasn't as comfortable with change as she had thought she was. "Nothing stayed the same for very long; it was very fast-moving, and change was really encouraged. . .it was my first opportunity to have to change a lot, and I wasn't very good at it. Working at Enron made me more adaptable and willing to change."

ENVIRONMENTAL CHANGES

Worrell had been working there for about a year when she noticed some abnormal behavior. "There were all these memos going around, and normally anybody could pick up a fax and take it over, because we are all HR and we have to be confidential, but the VPs would walk in to get their faxes right when faxes were coming in. We started thinking, something is going down."

A few weeks later her normally high-energy, stressful job abruptly changed. "They put a hiring freeze on everything at the beginning of October. So we couldn't hire anybody, which meant we didn't have anything to do. We finished up all the new hires that were currently open and we basically just sat around. We cleaned up our desks and got things organized and then we got to working on our résumés, because we thought, something's going on here and we need to be prepared."

A month later the news was announced to her department. "It was the beginning of November when they told us they were filing for bankruptcy, and that's when our bosses turned to us and said, 'Get your résumés ready, be prepared, start looking now if you have to.'"

A few of her co-workers felt confident their positions were secure, but Worrell didn't share their sentiment; she knew her days were numbered. "There were some people that were kind of cocky and said, 'Oh, if someone's got to go, it won't be me; they will want me!' I was not in that position. I was still very brand-new."

THE END IS HERE

On Monday, December 3, Worrell and her group came in to work expecting the worst. "On the last day we knew something was about to happen. . .they had given us the heads-up beforehand. Our immediate supervisors had said, 'Be prepared; Monday's not going to be a fun day, so really, just be prepared.'"

When Monday morning arrived, they were as ready as they could be. "Management got us together and said, 'You are going to be broken into groups and sent to each floor.' It was the generalists who did all the work in regards to laying people off. We went kind of as backup support."

Worrell and her group stood without emotion and bore witness to the largest layoff in American history. She was surprised at the directness of the conversation, but knew there was little else to say. "They said to them almost nothing, except 'Collect your things and leave and go home. If you get a callback you still have your job. If you don't, you don't.' I am abbreviating it, I know more words were in there, but that was really all I heard, and after talking to other people that worked there, that's really all they heard."

Everyone was left to pack up their things and say their goodbyes. Worrell and her group took the opportunity to document the day before returning to their office. "We all started taking pictures in front of the 'E.' Jesse Jackson was there, and a bunch of people went down and got their photograph taken with Jesse Jackson. . .We didn't know where we stood in all this at that point. We knew something was coming but we didn't know what."

A short while later, they looked on as everyone who was laid off evacuated the building. "You could see people leaving in droves, down the elevators with boxes and stuff. And then we went up to our desks."

The finality of the situation began to sink in as they waited for news of their fate. "After all of the staff had been notified, they came up to HR and said to us pretty much the same thing: 'We don't know anything, if you are going to get any money or not; we don't know what's going to happen.' It was up to the courts now, because they'd filed for bankruptcy. If you had already gotten a call, then you had your job. If you have not already gotten a call, then you were gone. So in HR, they had already notified the people who still had their jobs, instead of the reverse, which is what they did with the rest of the company."

As these last laid-off employees were notified, Worrell looked around and could see she was far more fortunate than others. "The saddest part for me was learning, because we had lots of people in our department who had spouses who also worked at Enron, that a whole family, the husband and wife, had both lost their jobs."

It was only 3:30 p.m. but it felt like it had taken all day. Over the previous few weeks Worrell had taken most of her things home and was down to one box. Emotionally exhausted, she left to face her future. "We collected ourselves and everybody wished each other well, and we exchanged information so we could stay in contact with one another. . . I got my box and I carried it out the front door.. . .But it's funny, because, to this day, when they talk about Enron and show footage, you see me carrying my box out."

A CHRISTMAS TO REMEMBER

Worrell was very active in her church and since October she had been preparing for the Christmas musical. "I was rehearsing a lot at night, and that helped to relieve some of the stress and anxiety. Being around and meeting new people and being in a Christian environment got me through Christmas. I had something to focus on. I didn't have to stay at home and be depressed; I had something to get me out, keep me involved. I was making new friends and it was a blessing for me to have all of that."

Worrell comes from a large family and Christmas is one of her favorite times of year. Her way of expressing and feeling love is through gifts—it is her love language—but she couldn't afford them this year. Complicating matters, her sister, who lived near her family in Vermont, was pregnant with her third child and due any time. "I couldn't afford to travel home, and I didn't want my family to spend their money on coming to see me. . .but they wanted us to be together. So they made a family decision to split us up. My dad and one of my brothers came here, and my mom, my grandmother, and one of my other brothers stayed with my sister so there was family with her when she had her child."

It touched her heart to have some immediate family close by on Christmas Day, but it wasn't the same. "I enjoyed having my dad and my brother here; we did our own little Christmas. I know for the future that my mom was the one that stuffed my stocking. My dad did it here; he tried real hard, but it wasn't the same."

LOOKING FOR WORK

Worrell immediately began looking for work. "I had no financial support. I hadn't saved up a whole lot, because I hadn't worked there long enough and I was fresh out of college. I was just learning how to manage my money and I needed a job as fast as possible."

Interviewing after Enron was uncomfortable at times. "They wanted to know if I knew any dirt, but they didn't question my role in anything. . .The first question anybody asked is, 'Did you know Ken Lay?' I still get that question to this day. Second question is usually, 'Were you told to shred documents?' That was funny to me because I'm in HR; we have to shred documents, they have personal information on them. We all had personal shredders under our desks. . .I would laugh at that question."

Worrell did know Kenneth Lay, sort of. They happened to attend the same church. From what she saw, he was a good and thoughtful man. "My aunt became a pastor and so I switched to her church and that was the church [Lay] was at. My aunt would joke with him and say, 'My son is still there, but my niece that got him his job is not there anymore.' She introduced me to him one day and he made a point of stopping me every time he saw me and asked, 'Have you found a job? How are you doing?' I felt like he genuinely cared, so to me that helped a lot."

Within about three weeks she found solid employment with a contingency recruiting agency which had worked with Enron. She knew a few recruiters had gone to work there after being laid off. With no other job prospects, she happily accepted the position. "I worked there for about six months. I will honestly say it was the worst job I had ever had. It was really hellish; she was not a fun person to work for. So I went from working in a really great company, Enron, where I felt like I had a family of people that cared about me and wanted me to succeed, to this woman who was self-centered, and all she cared about was getting a backrub when she got there first thing in the morning."

Worrell was not the only one to feel the culture shock. "It was this huge difference and the recruiters were miserable and I was miserable. I went through a depression and it was hard that first six months. I would say to myself, 'Why am I putting myself through this? Because I don't have a choice, I have to have a job.' I was not going to quit that job without another ready."

Emotionally beat down, she had no motivation to give as much to this company as she did Enron. "This woman had unrealistic expectations. What's funny, at Enron sometimes they too had some pretty unrealistic expectations, but you wanted to meet those expectations. At this place you didn't. It was so miserable you didn't want to do anything for her."

It wasn't as simple for Worrell as changing companies; outside agencies didn't readily hire support positions. She was going to have to find something completely unrelated, but soon realized that it wasn't as easy to get a job with Enron on your résumé. "It was hard to find a job as an Enron employee. It was believed that Enron paid above industry standards and that we expected more money coming into positions. People didn't even want to interview us because they thought, 'Well, we can't afford them,' when in all actuality, we just wanted jobs; they wouldn't even give us the opportunity to interview."

UNLIKELY OPPORTUNITIES

Being a part of the Enron group may have eliminated her from the general pool of candidates, but everyone in this tight-knit group really looked out for one another. "Everybody banded together to do what they could to help each other find another job. "I put feelers out with the Enron people that I knew."

A former co-worker let her know of a position that was to be opening up soon where she worked, "She said, 'You would love this company! There is an admin position coming up.'"

Worrell was less than excited when she heard about the position: an Administrative Assistant in the Finance Department wasn't exactly on her career plan. "I thought, 'I did not go to college for five years to get this degree to be an administrative assistant!' That was my first thought, and then I thought, 'What would it hurt to do the interview? I am so miserable in this job, even if it is a job that I think I wouldn't normally want to do, why not?'"

The offices are only open half days on Friday; at 12:30 p.m. Worrell was scheduled to come in for an interview. "I was there till 5:30. She and I started talking and she's got a lot of kids and I have a large family. . . At the end, she said, 'I have a couple more interviews next week and I will let you know sometime next week.'"

Worrell left feeling really good about the interview. Even though initially she wasn't interested, after meeting her potential boss, the idea of working for someone she actually liked meant more than a job title. Early the next morning Worrell received a surprising phone call from her interviewer. "She said, 'You know, I woke up this morning and I said I don't need to interview anyone else; you're the one we want.' So, she hired me."

Worrell went to her old boss and submitted her resignation first thing Monday morning. Her boss refused to accept the two-week notice. "She said, 'I don't want you working here anymore.' I stayed a week, I think, to clean some things up and then I left there; I had a week off before I started my next position."

ANSWERED PRAYERS

Working for her new boss was a breath of fresh air for Worrell. The work environment was similar to Enron in that she felt like part of a large family. She had been working there for over a year and began to feel hungry for a more challenging position. "I loved it, but I was bored."

One day she received a pamphlet in the mail about a non-profit organization funded by the company she works for. They offer grants to teachers for self-designed professional summer learning experiences. "I didn't know enough about it and I looked and thought, 'Oh this sounds cool, I will send it to my mom and let her know all the great things my company is doing for education.'"

Unfortunately the grants are available only to teachers who live within a specific geographical area and Vermont was not included. Even though her mom was not eligible, she was still very impressed with the program. "My mom thought it was great and she wrote an email to the founder thanking him for everything he was doing. He said she had spunk and wanted to give her money."

Those rules of eligibility were set in stone and not even the founder could break them. "He did give her money out of his own pocket, a grant out of his pocket. I went up to thank the Executive Director for the award, for giving it to my mother."

Worrell ended up talking to the director about the grant, and the conversation turned to her non-profit activities. The director was intrigued and remained in contact with Worrell. "One day we were talking, and she said, 'Are you happy in your position, or if something were to open up with the program would you be interested?' I said, 'Yeah, I would be interested!'"

Her heart leapt in her chest but before it took flight she received the bad news. She had never worked directly for a non-profit organization before and she would need to take a few courses at a local university to be eligible to apply for any position that might open up. "I thought, 'Oh this stinks, I can't afford those courses.'"

Crushed, Worrell went back to her job and began dis-cussing it with her boss in the finance department. "She said, 'Do you really want to do this? Because if this is really what you want, I will pay for your courses so you can move positions.'"

Worrell caught her breath. She was immediately overwhelmed with emotion and gratitude and without hesitation accepted the offer. It ended up changing her life and her career. "She did, she paid for me to go to the courses. . .When one of the positions came open, the woman who is now my boss, the executive director, hired me, and I've been there ever since."

Even though the Enron bankruptcy was the cause of her suffering, without it she would not be where she is today. "I've steadily moved up in responsibility, and I love it. It gives back to education. I always thought I wanted to be in the classroom, but I love being on the business side of things. I think one of the reasons why I love that is because of my time at Enron."

THE FINANCIAL IMPACT

It is a common belief by the general public that Enron coerced employees into buying stock. "I will say we weren't specifically told to buy stock; it was recommended. I would also say a lot of people were like, 'Why not?' Nobody really had an idea of really what was going on except those people who were doing it, and those around them; those of us who were lower and not involved at all in that area had no idea."

The stock kept rising and they knew people who were making serious money; it seemed like a sure investment. "Our company is doing great, why not put all our money in Enron stock?' Things were getting better and better and the reports we were getting at annual meetings were great. For me and some of my friends that worked there, it wasn't a matter of them dictating or saying that we had to, but they did make it sound like the most appealing option. In the end it was ultimately our choice."

Worrell was new to investing and losing everything when the stock crashed was a shock. "I grew up with people that are in education and the whole idea of stock was new to me. . .I had a considerable amount of stock, they give you a lot of stock, especially when you hire on. . .in the end I lost about $25,000, which for me was a lot. . .But knowing how much everybody lost, their whole life savings and their retirement, I thought, 'Oh, man, I am good.'"

REQUIRED GROWTH

Worrell was 24 when she was laid off from Enron. It was her first taste of making it on her own. "After college, I didn't have a job but I had the support of my parents, and after moving to Houston I pretty much found a position right away. So I never really had to flounder."

When she lost her job she had two choices: She could stay in Houston or go back home to Vermont. "It could have been really easy to give up and move home with my parents, try and let them support me, but I was making a life for myself here and I didn't want to have to do that. At the same time I was stressed, but I never felt worried and I think that was my faith. I'd always been taught that God will provide. I know that doesn't mean I can sit back and He will bring money down from the heavens, but I was never worried that I wasn't going to make it."

In the end she learned what she was capable of doing. "I realized I can survive. For me, it was a growing moment, because I persevered and I didn't break down. I battled depression afterwards; I still pulled through, I didn't give up. . .When I persevered, that strengthened my faith, because I said to myself, 'See God will provide; see, I am good! When I had weak moments I would pray or go to church, so my faith got me through a lot of it, and the support of my friends and family."

Worrell credits Enron for giving her the life she enjoys today. "I am still friends with a lot of people that I worked with at Enron. . .My life now is a huge result of the time I spent there and would be completely different had I not."

WORDS OF ADVICE

Expand your network. "Your network is your most valuable asset, be it looking for a job, getting into a new church or whatever. Use social media, a friend of a friend, expand your network. It will help you no matter what the situation."

FOR THOSE FACING A LAYOFF

Ready your résumé. "Keep the résumé simple and concise. Sometimes more is just more, it's not better. For a lot of people, the first thing they see is the first couple of sentences and if it doesn't catch their interest they will throw it away; focus on the beginning."

" I didn't see it then, but it turned out that getting fired from Apple was the best thing that could have ever happened to me. The heaviness of being successful was replaced by the lightness of being a beginner again, less sure about everything. It freed me to enter one of the most creative periods of my life."

-Steve Jobs

JIM ROUNTREE

HOUSTON, TEXAS – 4 YEARS

*J*im Rountree was working for on a pipeline project between Illinois and Canada when the opportunity to work for Enron materialized. He recognized there was a demand for emergency preparedness in the pipeline industry and began asking if anyone knew of anyone hiring. A co-worker urged him to contact Enron. A few phone calls later and he found himself a candidate for a position they were looking to fill. "I heard about it in August or September; by December I had the job."

The opportunity was beyond anything Rountree had ever hoped for. "I moved down there in January and started working. I commuted in on the bus every day in the beginning because you don't make enough at universities to do anything; this new job more than doubled my salary from the university. It wasn't a question of whether or not I was going to go; I had a wife and two kids. I was more than excited and probably in a state of euphoric denial of any other thing going on around me. It was all about me and I couldn't believe it."

ADJUSTING TO ENRON

Rountree was hired as Enron's Corporate Crisis Manager. His position required constant travel throughout the world. "I was gone all the time."

After his first month at Enron, Rountree received his first corporate American Express bill. Unsure of the procedures, he took it to his assistant and asked how to submit it for reimbursement. Rountree asked, "'Now what do we do with expense reports?' And she goes, 'I'll do that for you.' She took that expense report out of my hand and I never saw it again. Then one day one or two weeks later a check for that amount came and paid off the card. . . I couldn't believe it."

It wasn't so much the amount of money involved, it was the availability of the money. He had never experienced such financial freedom in a workplace environment before. His previous employer was a very conservative university that made sure every cent was accounted for; it was a definite culture shock coming to work for Enron. "When I worked at the university and we traveled, I was given a per diem of $75 a day. That $75 had to cover your hotel room and your meal. You are eating three meals a day; you are staying at the La Quinta and taking the State of Texas rate so you can have enough to eat your dinner."

Rountree was finally free of the confines of bureaucracy and budget constraints. He could now focus his attention on his job and not worry about how he was going to find the money to fund the project. "I never worried about an expense report; I never had an expense denied. I was questioned, I had a very attentive boss, but he questioned to the extent that expenses were allowed by the company. He never said anything, but if I needed something and could justify it doing my job, it was never questioned, ever."

It didn't take long to get used to this new lifestyle. "I walked into this and it was a complete change in the paradigm of living that I was used to. It wasn't the money; it was the apparent unending supply of it. You got used to it very quickly. You walked in and anything that you wanted or anything that you needed was at your disposal; you became accustomed to that very quickly, and so you fell in line."

He had come from a state university with strict budget limits, being a government employee, to Enron, where money was a tool and spent, any amount necessary, to get the job done. He could now "pick up the phone and ask my boss and get what I needed right away."

THE BEST PLACE TO WORK

It was an amazing place to work; everyone loved their jobs because they were allotted the resources to do their jobs well. "This is the other side of the dynamic at Enron. Despite all the money that wasn't questioned, that also led to a burden-free environment. You were able to be creative not worrying about these things; in fact, we were overly creative. You had time and energy and because you didn't worry about anything else, you enjoyed going and doing what you were doing."

In addition to the worry-free working environment, many were making more money than they had ever seen before in their lives. "I knew plenty of people who, during the course of their jobs, were consistently watching their stock value; they were past the point of being well-to-do. These were people who were millionaires, some of them many times over. It was so different to be in an organization like that. It was almost like the money was free-flowing, and they didn't know where it was coming from."

Because every day was a party, few had reason to care about the mechanics behind the machine. "I think everybody thought we sold oil, and energy, and futures, but the reality is I'm not sure many people knew exactly what we did, because so many things lost money and we knew very little about the ones that made money. And of course you don't promote the ones that lose money, and if you're not making money, you promote the name and not the fact that it's not making money. . .It wasn't a conspiracy to keep you from knowing anything, it was just the way it was managed—you really came to believe money was nothing there."

LOOKING BEHIND THE SCENES

Rountree visited the power plant Enron was building in India. "A major thing that I will never forget is that the water cooling tower that supplied all the cooling for these really expensive turbines that were being built. . .and I walked straight to the tower and climbed up to the top and the metal walk-across grate was so rusted through that it was in danger of structural failure in some places. . . Every electrical switch and whatnot was completely corroded, thoroughly."

The project was still under construction and Rountree was shocked at how little was being done to preserve the investment. "That type of thing I saw in a number of different places. But there were oversights because people were focused on the project. . .but the sustainability of that project and its long term viability, it was almost like it didn't exist. . .It made me realize that their focus was on driving this company forward. . .It's great for your stockholders, but it's terrible for your long-term viability."

Enron was also building a power plant in the Gaza Strip. Rountree was sent to help evacuate expatriates who were working for Enron because the Intifada had started back up again and their lives were in danger due to sporadic fighting and attacks near the project site. "When you looked at where the power plant was located, it was in the most dangerous place around. It was like putting a giant fuel tank with a big X on it for an Israeli fighter to come over and hit. Even though we were neutral, there were things that they were doing that were huge, in terms of geo-politics and their impact."

The entire project was a crisis manager's worst nightmare. "You have to ask yourself, is there really money in building a power plant in the Gaza Strip? I don't know the answer to that but it looked to me like it was a highly risky project. . .I thought, 'Okay, so the Palestinians will have a power plant, but in order to get fuel for that power plant or water or anything else, it has to come across Israeli territory."

SEEING THE END

Around September of 2001, Rountree began to suspect something was wrong at Enron. Although his position never allowed him to be privy to specific information, it wasn't hard to put together the pieces. "I know by looking at them, by how they acted, their body language. . .We were right under the 50th floor; we heard everything that went on."

"I heard their direct and indirect comments. I knew all the weaknesses; one of my jobs was to know what the weaknesses were. I knew that people brought up these things in risk sessions where we would sit around and talk about crisis risks from various points of view, and I knew what these crisis risks were. . .I knew the infrastructure and how some of these projects were losing money hand over fist, and there was no end in sight for when they were actually going to make money. You put it all together, and you say, 'The company's going to go down; it's just not going to go back up.'"

As time went on and Rountree learned more, he realized there was no saving Enron. "I think I was resigned that the corporation was going to fall probably before they actually started approaching other people about mergers. I remember thinking, 'Nobody's going to want this, no way. It's just not going to happen.'"

Rountree knew there was only a small group of people who really knew what was going on. One day he asked the question that weighed most on his mind. "I asked one fellow in the hall, I said, 'How is this going to end?' He looked straight back at me said, 'Badly,' and that was it."

Close to the end, Enron was constantly in the news, and none of it was good. "Their reputation was so far down the tubes at that point, it would have taken an insane amount of advertising and public relations money. . .to ever have come back from that."

Rountree was in the worst position; he knew the potential outcome but was unable to warn anyone else. "That would have been the end of me had I gone around saying, 'Well, in my opinion the company is going to fail.' What would that do for anybody else? That would just cause them to be in a more anxious state. Some might go out and be proactively looking for jobs, but most are just going to be paranoid and not enjoy whatever they have left. It wouldn't have made any difference. And after all, it was my opinion. . .So, you just sit around and watch."

Although he kept his concerns to himself, after the merger dissolved everyone else came to the same conclusion. "I guess the bad part of that whole experience came not necessarily when everyone was locked out of their retirement accounts. I think the bad part came psychologically for everybody in the company when it really dawned on them that this wasn't something that was just an anxiety issue; this was definitely going to happen. When that finally sank in, that was when the sick feelings started hitting everybody."

CLOSING ENRON'S DOORS

In preparation for the layoffs, the decision was made not to stop any employee from taking property belonging to Enron. "Number one, what were they protecting anyway? Number two, you are going to provoke something because somebody is going to say, 'Let me get this right, this corporation stole a million dollars from me and you are going to tell me that I can't have the flat-screen monitor that is sitting on my desk and my computer?'"

"Now a lot of people turned all their stuff in, but I personally knew people who kept their laptops when they left. They just walked with their laptops and anything else that they wanted and went right out the door. That was it. It was with an air of indignity and 'I dare you stop me.'. . . The only thing to be accomplished that day was to make sure that nobody got hurt and there was no violence. To make sure that everybody got home safe that night."

Rountree and his team knew they too were about to be laid off. "We all knew what everyone else knew, we were in no different boat, we were just employed for seven days longer, but I don't think we got any extra money for that. . .

We were actually working for money that we either wouldn't get or wasn't going to be there. But there was a camaraderie amongst my group. We all did the same type of things so it was kind of an acceptance of what was going to happen. It was benign. It was like a bunch of soldiers doing their job and trying not to have any type of feelings about it because it wouldn't do any good."

When the last day came for Rountree, he remembers thinking while he walked out of the building, "That this was all sad, but my thought was, 'I just saw history. I just lived and saw history.' That is what it was. When I left, I saw history and how grateful I was to have been in the middle of it and have seen it firsthand."

THE FINANCIAL IMPACT

Rountree had most of his retirement invested in Enron stock. It still pains Rountree when he thinks about what he lost. "I feel a little negligent. I knew better than to keep everything I had wrapped up in it. . .I honestly don't remember how much I lost. If I had to hazard a guess, I'd say probably around $100,000."

The money never seemed real to him because most of it was money he never touched and had no intention of touching for many years to come. He knew at his age it was likely that he would eventually overcome that loss; he saw no benefit in worrying about it. "I don't look back with any type of bitterness. But again, here's the thing: I didn't lose twenty years; I lost two or three. It wasn't a significant investment for a mid-thirties guy with a wife, two kids and a house."

Rountree considers himself very fortunate. "I would have paid Enron for the experience that I got. And I knew that at the time. I would have done that work for free. Because I learned more in the time that I was there than I could have in a lifetime of what I was doing or what I've done since. I have never been able to gain that amount of experience in that short of period of time and I don't ever see it ever happening again. It was unbelievable. And because of that, I know that my life today is directly related to getting hired there. I knew that when I went to work there it was going to change my life; I knew it, and it did without a doubt."

It also helped that he was entertaining job offers immediately after the bankruptcy was announced. "There were so many opportunities that I felt like I didn't want to go to any one particular position. I said, 'This is enough to start a business. I can use the collapse of Enron, having been in the middle of it, and help people put in place measures to keep this from happening to them.' That was a real value in the world at that time."

Through it all, he knew to let it go and move on. "It failed and I couldn't do anything about it. It was beyond my capability to manage it, so if I couldn't do anything about it then there's no sense in worrying about it; I would just look towards the future and go on. I knew to do that. A lot of people didn't. It wasn't because people had started offering me jobs at that point; that happened towards the end. Of course you get the anxiety, I went through anxiety just like everyone else did, but it wasn't the end of the world."

Without Enron he wouldn't have the life he has today. "It has never been the same since. With that being said, I have made more money every year than I ever made there. It was almost like a school for me. Every year after that has been better than any year I had at Enron. . .I would have never had that opportunity had I not been there until the end. Watching what was going on, being in the middle of it all, watching it happen, not being a decision-maker but carrying out and executing other people's decisions. It was the best experience I have ever had; it was invaluable."

A REASON TO BELIEVE

Rountree knew there was little about the situation that he could control so he didn't worry about it. His training has ingrained in him that any situation, regardless of how dire, can always be worse. "I always look at it like this and say, 'Man this could've been a lot worse.' Part of this is my training and experience and studying years of disasters and knowing that things can always be worse. Because I know that and because I believe the way I believe, it is easier to take these types of things."

As a strong Christian, Rountree used his faith to help guide him through this unusual time. "Spirituality is a key for me anyway. I don't know what it is like not to be spiritual. The whole experience since then has cemented in my faith and what I believe, but it wasn't dependent upon it. Faith was a way to get through it, but it wasn't a crutch. It was something I had before, but I just even explored it further after the fact."

Rountree believes that his success today is directly tied to his faith. "I spend time in prayer, and at the time really trusted God that I'd end up in the right place, and every time I have trusted, I wound up in the right place without question, so I trust and go forward. There is a line in a song that I repeat in my head a lot. . .'Do your best, pray that it's blessed and He'll take care of the rest.' It's really true; what else can you do but your best?"

He warns that simply believing isn't enough; God needs to be an integral part of your life in order for Him to be able to influence it. "I hesitate to say it with such totality, because if you take someone who is not a believer and tell them this is the way out and they don't have some experience behind their spirituality to understand it, it adds to the burden. . .God was not the way out of it. God was the reason why I was there and God was the reason why I left."

The group he worked with was especially close-knit as they usually spent many hours together on overseas projects. It was not uncommon for them to converse on various subjects, including spiritual beliefs. Looking at who they are today, he sees a connection. "I don't know of a single case of a nonbeliever or agnostic type that was able to do, within the same period of time or with the grace or apparent ease as the people that I am thinking about, they just weren't able to do it. The ones who were spiritually-based, by far and away, shone above everyone else whom I knew that wasn't."

A WORD OF ADVICE

Be financially responsible. "Getting fired isn't anything. If you got yourself into a financial position to where you can't take that hit and go on indefinitely, then you have mismanaged not the money that you have but the life you've been leading."

Help those in need. "Look for someone in need and wonder if I might provide some relief from that, in one way or another."

Have an accountability partner. "Everybody is accountable to somebody, and if you don't have anyone in your life that you are accountable to, or if you're not accountable to God, my opinion is that you are wandering without purpose and you are not living up to your potential. You have to be accountable to someone or something to keep yourself in check. There is no way to measure the progress of your life or the value of what you are doing if you're not accountable to someone; you need to find someone to be accountable to."

Admit your faults. "The more I talk to my kids, the more I try to make them realize that I am not a superhero; I'm their dad and I have as many faults as everybody else out there. If you can learn from my faults, great! I think what happens in a lot of cases is that the parents point out all their children's faults while refusing to acknowledge any of their own."

FOR THOSE FACING A LAYOFF

Be open about what you are going through. "Be with other people. Don't be alone, talk to other people, don't withdraw and don't go into a hole. Share your concerns, share your worries with other people, and if you don't already, you will soon discover that every emotion you have is shared by everyone around you. And the ones that appear the most stalwart are often the ones who are the most vulnerable and torn up, and you would never know it."

Find a support group. "It's all about honesty, openness, and transparency, about the way that you feel that gets people through this thing. If you need to go to a group and talk about this with other people that are going the same thing, I would do it. . . .Be around other people who have had similar experiences who can share what they did to get over it."

Try to stay optimistic for your family. "Your children and your spouse are going to pick up the exact same attitude that you have. If you are around them moping every day about not having a job and doomsday, you can bet your wife and kids are going through an equal amount of stress, all of the time not wanting to show you their concern for fear that they might upset you even more."

Move on and let the past go. "It's hard to appreciate what you have until it's taken away from you. Letting it be taken away from you and rolling with it is a learning experience in itself. To fight it, knowing you can't win, is a waste of time and effort that could be best spent rebuilding your life elsewhere."

Be confident in yourself. "When you realize your worth isn't based on what other people think, but on your ability to adapt to the situations presented to you with the right mental attitude and frame, then you realize that that's the ticket and the rest is a lie. It's almost like somebody just pulled a cover off of all the opportunities. When you quit thinking about and dwelling about the bad, you're able to see the good."

Use the messages found in this book. "Don't read it as a motivational book, but read it as a book on how to survive. It's more a survival book. This is how I survived, this how my friends survived, this is how we survived. We don't know how you are going to survive, but if we can help you through sharing some of our personal moments, maybe you might not have to go through some of the angst that we went through. . .This book is not about Enron; it's just about people."

Share this book with others. "If you actually had the courage to pick up this book, try to find someone who's been laid off that doesn't have the courage or can't find the will to get out of bed. Go talk to them. Because if you have the strength to buy this book, you might have the strength to help somebody else get to the same place you are, or just get out of bed."

ABOUT THE AUTHOR

Carey Falter is a freelance writer, poet and a professional homemaker. Born and raised in southern Arizona, she is a graduate of the University of Arizona's Eller College of Business. In addition to her other freelance activities, she writes business book summaries for EBSCO Publishing. She is a proud member of the Catholic Church, a devoted wife, and a mother of two wonderful boys.

ABOUT THE COVER ARTIST

The cover and interior page layout designer, Tamian Wood, winner of the 17th Annual Florida Print Awards, Best of Category, is currently based out of sunny South Florida. Using art, photography, typography and digital collage techniques, she creates book covers that appeal to the eye and the mind, to entice the book browser to become a book reader. She holds degrees in Computer Science and Graphic Design, and is a proud member of Phi Theta Kappa National Honour Society.

If you have a graphic design project that needs to be noticed, contact Tamian at designer@tamianwood.com. To find out more about the broad range of her design experience visit: http://www.tamianwood.com.